Contents

UK Edition

Copyright © 2016 text AG&G Books

The right of A. & G. Bridgewater to be identified as authors of this work has been asserted by them in accordance with the Copyright, Designs and Patents Act 1988.

Copyright © 2016 illustrations and photographs IMM Lifestyle Books

Copyright © 2016 IMM Lifestyle Books

Designed and created for IMM Lifestyle Books by AG&G Books. Copyright © 2004, 2016 "Specialist" AG&G Books

Design: Glyn Bridgewater; Illustrations: Gill Bridgewater; Editor: Alison Copland; Photographs: iStockphoto

Current Printing (last digit)

10 9 8 7 6 5 4 3

Printed in Malaysia

Home Gardener's No-Dig Raised Bed Gardens: Growing vegetables, salads and soft fruit in raised no-dig beds is published by Creative Homeowner under license with IMM Lifestyle Books.

ISBN: 978-1-58011-780-7

Creative Homeowner®, www.creativehomeowner.com, is distributed exclusively in the United Kingdom by Grantham Book Service, Trent Road, Grantham, Lincolnshire, NG31 7XQ.

We are always looking for talented authors. To submit an idea, please send a brief inquiry to acquisitions@foxchapelpublishing.com.

Author's foreword

A big garden in the country, a small garden in the town, a concrete slab garden on an industrial estate, a run-down allotment plot, a scrubland garden by the sea, a rock-strewn garden – no matter what your scenario is, if you have ambitions to grow your own organic vegetables a no-dig raised bed garden is the best way forward. The initial set-up will involve you in the sometimes sweat-making effort of drawing up plans, building beds, bringing in farmyard manure and spent mushroom compost, enclosing the whole area with a fence, and so on, but once you have the no-dig system up and running it will be a relatively smooth and easy ride. Just imagine … no more heavy, back-breaking slog with a spade, no more double digging, no more thinking about the qualities of the underlying base soil, no more spending ten years trying to improve the soil, no more chemical cure-alls, and hardly any weeding. The no-dig system of growing vegetables has everything going for it. If you go one step further and keep chickens, compost all your own kitchen waste, and use some part of your paper waste to make a mulch, then you will be able to achieve a tight, self-contained, eco-friendly system that will give you maximum output for minimum input. As for the frequently asked question of how long it will be before you are eating your own produce, the simple answer is that as soon the beds are in place you will be ready to get growing.

About the authors

Alan and Gill Bridgewater have gained an international reputation as producers of highly successful gardening and DIY books on a range of subjects, including garden design, ponds and patios, stone and brickwork, decks and decking, and household woodworking. They have also contributed to several international magazines. They live in Rye, East Sussex.

Measurements

Both metric and imperial measurements are given in this book – for example, 1.8 m (6 ft).

SEASONS

This book is aimed at readers worldwide, so seasons rather than months are used – early spring, mid-spring and so on. Although advice is given on the best time to sow, plant, tend and gather, because of regional variations you will have to be flexible and ready to modify dates to suit the mini climates that may exist in your area. In some northerly areas, spring may begin several weeks later than in more southerly regions.

Benefits of the no-dig method

No-dig gardening is an organic system that allows you to grow vegetables and other plants in raised beds without the need for any back-breaking digging, and without having to 'improve' the underlying natural soil in your garden. You can control the quality and depth of the growing medium in the raised beds and reduce the amount of work required to keep them free of weeds, pests and diseases.

What is no-dig gardening?

NO DIGGING

The no-dig system allows and encourages worms and other soil life to carry out the cultivation operations. Mulches of garden compost, farm manure, leafmould and other organic materials are layered up in raised beds in such a way that there is a reduction in pests, diseases and weeds, and an increase in beneficial soil fungi, worms, insects and microbes. This system might sound a bit too clever, but it is exactly how nature works: vegetation falls to the ground, worms and other soil organisms drag the organic matter down into the soil thereby enriching it, new plants grow, and so on.

HARDLY ANY WEEDING

There is an old adage that says 'one year's weed seeds means seven years' digging' – if you allow weeds to seed, you will be shackled by seven years of back-breaking digging and weeding. The no-dig system, however, sidesteps the whole problem of weeding by burying the seeds under layers of mulch. The undisturbed weed seeds are never given the chance to germinate.

SAVING EFFORT

In traditional vegetable cultivation you spend a huge amount of effort digging the whole plot, and then waste a good part of your efforts by walking over and compacting at least a third of the ground that you have painstakingly dug. With the no-dig raised bed system, the layout of paths and beds is permanent. Once the infrastructure is in place, you only need to expend effort on the growing areas within the beds.

PERFECT BALANCE

The no-dig system allows the population of beneficial soil life – worms, insects, microbes and fungi – to build up in such a way that a natural undisturbed environment is created in the important upper soil layers, with the effect of achieving a positive balance.

The no-dig system of raised beds and paths enables easy access to your crops.

MORE BENEFITS OF THE NO-DIG SYSTEM

- The height of the beds and the width of the paths can be tailored to suit your unique physical needs – for example, if you are in a wheelchair or are unable to bend.

- Higher crop yields are produced on a smaller ground area.

- The underlying soil and the layered growing medium within the beds remain undisturbed.

- More water and organic matter are retained in the growing medium.

- The structure and make-up of the growing medium within each bed can be targeted to suit specific plants.

- Beds can be designed to be hot, cool or deep.

- The narrow width of the beds means that you never have to walk on the planted area, and never have too far to stretch.

- The structure of the beds more easily allows the use of nets, windbreaks, plastic sheeting and fleece.

Raised bed options

What is the best material for raised beds?

Raised beds are essential in this system because they define and separate the growing and walking areas, and enable the gardener to control the quality of the growing medium by layering up organic matter within the beds. The height of the beds can also be modified to increase or decrease the depth of the growing medium, as required for different crops. The beds can be made from a variety of different materials.

THE POSSIBILITIES

Although there are many options – you could build raised beds in metal, wood, plastic, brick, stone, woven willow, straw bales, old lorry tyres or whatever else you can find (some of these are easier on the eye than others) – the two key thoughts here are that the structure of the beds should be long-lasting, and the design should be adaptable so that the beds can be stacked and/or moved. Woven willow looks good, but it is fragile and not easily adapted. Brick beds, on the other hand, certainly look good and they are long-lasting, but they are so fixed in form that they cannot be modified. While large lorry tyres last for ever and they can be stacked, they fail because the cavities hold too much water and give home to pests such as ants and mice. Look at the materials available in your area, and design the beds accordingly.

A bed made from readily available planed and treated softwood is a swift but expensive option.

You must think very long and hard before opting to build a long-lasting but inflexible brick bed.

Above: A long, deep bed made from thick-section treated softwood.

Left: Beds made from railway sleepers are long-lasting, flexible and good on the eye.

A extra long bed made from treated thick-section softwood – it is not very attractive, but is wonderfully practical.

A runner bean bed with a removable top section and a fixed central pole.

A builders' dumpy bag makes a swift and efficient temporary bed.

This bed has been made from the top section of a salvaged galvanized water butt.

The various photographs here will show you that there are indeed many possibilities, but you still must be mindful that if you really want to get the best out of a no-dig raised bed garden – maximum crops for minimum effort – then function is all-important. For this reason, a pattern of stackable wooden raised beds, as shown on page 13, with the addition of recycled dustbins and builders' 'dumpy' or 'jumbo' bags to be used as fill-in standbys, works extremely well. For example, if you decide to trial a new crop in a little-used marginal area of your plot, you could use a mix of dumpy bags and salvaged metal dustbins before going to the effort and expense of building a more permanent wooden bed.

Buildings and equipment

Awater butt and a shed for your gardening tools are both essential. There is no reason why you cannot manage without extras such as greenhouses and polytunnels, but if you have room for them they will make life easier in your no-dig garden. It is a pleasure to work in a warm, cosy greenhouse or polytunnel, especially when the weather is wet and windy, and they will allow you to extend the growing season.

What equipment will I need?

A polytunnel is a great option if you have the space and the money.

SOME BASIC EQUIPMENT

A selection of tools and materials you are likely to need is illustrated below. Buckets, old metal dustbins and more nets may be a useful addition to this list, and, if you can afford it, a large woodchipping machine would be a good option.

Collecting rainwater

If you have a shed, or your no-dig plot is close to the house, then one or more water butts, old tin baths, tanks or other receptacles to catch the rainwater are vital. There is no doubt that an ugly mix of butts, baths and buckets looks a bit of a mess, but they are a wonderful way of saving water, and they really come into their own when you want to puddle in seedlings without going to all the bother of turning on the mains taps. Before setting out rain barrels, make sure they are allowed by your local codes.

TOOLS

Spade • Fork • Rake • Hoe • Dibber • Secateurs • Trowel • Hand fork • Loppers

Pegs and string • Scissors • Gloves • Plastic netting • Canes

Bubble wrap • Fleece

Bucket • Watering-can • Wheelbarrow • String

GARDEN SHED

No doubt you could leave your tools and materials in various corners of the garage or house, but in practice a dedicated garden shed is best. The ideal shed will have a bench on one side, an old armchair, natural light, plenty of hooks and shelves to hold and contain your tools and materials, a radio, a power point so that you can make tea or coffee, a calendar, a pad and a pencil, and so on. Remember that a shed is more than just a place to store your things – it is also a place where you can just sit and contemplate.

GREENHOUSES AND POLYTUNNELS

Every no-dig grower of vegetables, no matter how small their plot, needs some means of raising, growing on and hardening off plants so that they are ready for planting out in the open. This is even more important if you want to extend the growing season. Plastic-covered frames, hotbeds with some sort of frame over them, cloches, fleeces, nets and so on are all good options – but, when you really get down to it, the ideal is to have a greenhouse or, better still, a polytunnel.

GREENHOUSES

While any greenhouse is better than nothing, the ultimate is to have a traditional cedarwood greenhouse set on a low brick wall. Wood can easily be mended and modified, and the bricks hold in the warmth of the sun. Such a greenhouse will also need an area of slatted staging at table level, and a selection of shelves. Most greenhouses are limited in size and shape, however, so they are really only good for sowing, potting on, and growing pot-grown crops.

POLYTUNNELS

A polytunnel can be used – because of its size and shape and the way the ends can be opened up to the air – for sowing seeds, potting on, growing various plants prior to planting them out, growing crops like tomatoes, sweet peppers and cucumbers, and growing a whole range of salad leaf crops directly in beds. This versatility gives them the advantage over a greenhouse. They allow you to work in wet and windy weather, and to plant early and crop late.

OPTIONS

A good part of the pleasure of designing, building and working a no-dig raised bed garden is figuring out just how to use found and salvaged materials to combat and beat the weather – to protect against wind, to shelter from frost, to capture the heat from the sun, and generally to create the best environment for the plants. If you enjoy recycling and salvaging materials, and generally playing around with hammers, nails and string, then you will have a great time.

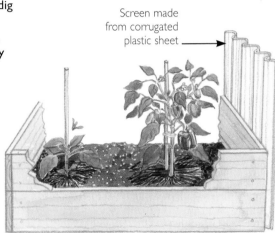

Screen made from corrugated plastic sheet →

A bed designed specifically to nurture delicate plants. The deep sides protect from blustery winds and the screen makes the most of the sun.

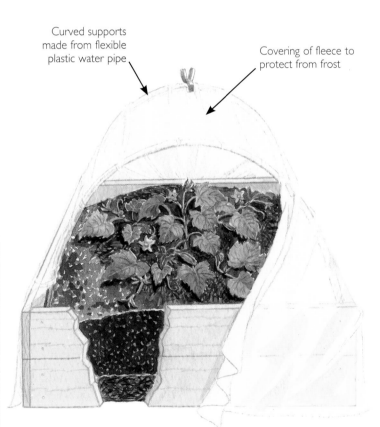

Curved supports made from flexible plastic water pipe

Covering of fleece to protect from frost

A bed designed with removable frames that allow for extra deep mulches. The idea is that you can sit an extra frame in place, add more mulch, fit another frame, and so on, to suit the growing depth of the plant.

Screen made from sticks, string and plastic sheet

A small bed with a screen made and positioned to suit – either to keep off the wind or to focus the rays of the sun onto the growing crop.

The perfect plot

T**he wonderful thing about no-dig raised bed vegetable gardening is that you can, to a great extent, ignore the make-up of the basic natural soil. Certainly, you would need to drain a wet site, and you still have to think about how the plot relates to the sun and to large trees or other obstructions such as outbuildings, but at least you do not have to think about the quality of the soil and/or digging it.**

What makes the perfect plot?

Checklist

- The ideal is to have either a level or a gently sloping site that faces the sun at midday.

- It is best if the plot is protected to the windward side – with trees or rising ground to keep off the prevailing winds.

- Good free drainage is important – avoid a site that looks in any way damp, or smells sour.

- You need one or more standpipes – so that you can rig up a sprinkler watering system.

- Make sure if you aim to have a greenhouse and/or polytunnel that there is enough room to site them at the back of the plot – so that they get the sun without casting a shadow over the rest of the plot.

- Make sure there is enough room for a shed – so that you can put it well away from the beds and it will not cast a shadow over them.

- If you have a long, narrow garden with high walls to the sunny side, site the beds on the side away from the walls so they make the most of the sun.

- If you have a very large garden in the country, so that you can more or less design the garden to suit, have two gates so that you can push carts, trolleys or barrows in through one gate and out through the other.

- Try to avoid trees or large shrubs that might suck water out of the ground and/or shed leaves over the beds.

- If you have a large garden and intend keeping chickens, ducks or geese to give you manure, try to arrange the set-up so that you keep the distance between the poultry shed and the vegetable garden to the minimum.

A plot in its early stages – note the netting to protect from frost, the recycled galvanized water butts, and the black plastic sheet that will eventually be covered in wood chippings.

TOWN PLOT

A town garden is fine, as long as you dedicate the whole area to the no-dig system, because a no-dig raised bed system works best when all the elements are shaped and positioned for the common no-dig good. For example, imagine a small town garden scenario where the family – mum, dad and two children – have six raised beds in the front garden, and a dozen or so beds and four chickens in an ark in the back garden. There is not much lawn, but the kids are so involved with the fun of it all that they do not really need a big play area.

VILLAGE PLOT

A village plot is a good option in that, to a great extent, the whole rural community set-up tends to be in tune with nature. Imagine a village scenario where mum, dad and four children live in a large end-terrace house where they have a huge corner plot plus a strip of allotment at the far end of the garden. They have a massive system of beds that covers just about the whole garden. They have chickens, an old greenhouse and a very long polytunnel. Their plot is so productive that they also sell produce at the gate. Villagers pop in and buy fresh eggs, vegetables and fruit – anything that is in season.

COUNTRY PLOT

The very best option is a virgin plot in the country. Right from the start you can stake out what you think is the perfect arrangement of beds and take it from there. There may be overhanging trees, slopes and other problems, but if you are starting from scratch you can easily work round these. You may subsequently need to make changes to the height of the beds, the position of gates and other items, but that is all part of the fun.

THE IDEAL NO-DIG PLOT

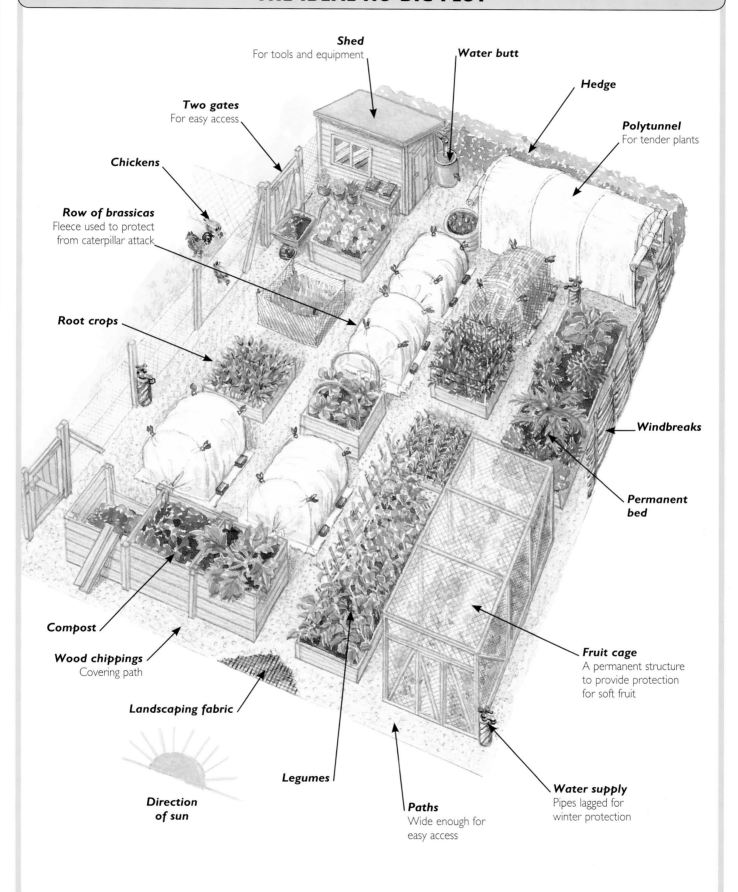

Shed
For tools and equipment

Water butt

Hedge

Polytunnel
For tender plants

Two gates
For easy access

Chickens

Row of brassicas
Fleece used to protect
from caterpillar attack

Root crops

Windbreaks

**Permanent
bed**

Compost

Wood chippings
Covering path

Landscaping fabric

**Direction
of sun**

Legumes

Paths
Wide enough for
easy access

Fruit cage
A permanent structure
to provide protection
for soft fruit

Water supply
Pipes lagged for
winter protection

Small gardens

Is no-dig possible in a small garden?

There are examples of communal no-dig gardens on the flat roofs of high-rise blocks, productive set-ups in minute front gardens, beautifully inventive beds made of corrugated sheet, and gardens built and stepped like a Mayan ruin – all designed to make the most of limited space. If you are keen and inventive, there are endless possibilities for creating a no-dig system in your small garden. Here are a few ideas.

A small garden in town where railway sleepers have been used to build a mix of beds, steps, walls and patios.

CONCRETE GARDEN

A couple moved into a property where the garden was full of concrete slabs and corrugated-iron Nissan-hut-type buildings that had been used as chicken sheds. They simply dismantled the buildings, rebolted the corrugated iron together to make raised beds, set the beds in place on the concrete slabs, filled them up with the well-rotted chicken manure that littered the site, and began planting.

POLYTUNNEL GARDEN

Another couple moved into a village property where the long, thin garden was mostly taken up by a huge polytunnel (probably part of some long-gone nursery). They built an arrangement of raised beds in the polytunnel, rigged up as many shelves and hanging baskets as the structure would hold, and gave the rest of the garden over to chickens. It is intensive and a bit smelly, but it works for them.

JUNKYARD GARDEN

An old couple moved into a country property where the garden was packed full of large wooden packing cases, pallets and stacks of old lorry tyres. It was a complete junkyard. They stacked the tyres three deep to make raised beds, turned the pallet and packing cases into more beds and a couple of chicken sheds, begged horse manure from the local stables, and then got on with rearing chickens and planting up the raised beds. It is not very pretty, but its productivity and order make the garden special.

Small garden solutions

- You could be single-minded, clear out everything and dedicate the whole plot and all your spare energy to using every bit of available space.

- You could approach the local community council and see if they have any available funds, or perhaps even a patch of vacant ground.

- You could double your space by building stepped beds, meaning that you grow some crops such as salad leaves, herbs and tomatoes on special frames, wall boxes and racks.

- You could join forces with a neighbour and divide the whole project into tasks – building beds, keeping poultry, sowing, planting – and then split the work according to your needs and pleasures.

- You could join forces with several neighbours to create a mini smallholding with lots of chickens and a large polytunnel. In this way you could maximize your output and completely take up any gluts.

- You could join forces with an aged neighbour – you take over their plot and in exchange you give them as much produce as they need.

- You could join forces with a physically disabled neighbour – you take over their garden and build beds that are wheelchair accessible, and in return you divide the produce.

- You could join forces with a neighbour who hates gardening but enjoys indoor activities such as cooking – you take over their plot, you split the produce and they turn some of the produce into jams, preserves, frozen vegetables and so on.

PLANNING A SMALL NO-DIG RAISED BED GARDEN

Walk around your garden at various times, at sunrise and sunset and in various weather conditions, and consider carefully how the season of the year, time of day and weather conditions all affect the space. Look at the width and length of the garden, the height of boundary walls and fences, the shape of the plot in relation to tall trees and neighbouring buildings, and think it all through. Do you want to turn the whole space into a no-dig garden with a range of raised beds and a poultry run, or do you simply want to set a single small area aside? Consider how friends and family use the space. Take everything into account, then draw up a design.

SMALL GARDEN DESIGNS

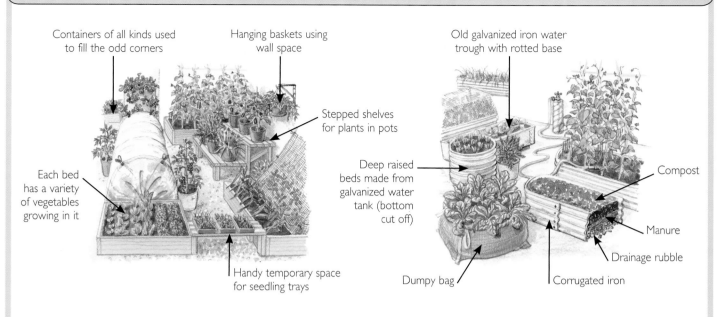

Containers of all kinds used to fill the odd corners

Hanging baskets using wall space

Old galvanized iron water trough with rotted base

Stepped shelves for plants in pots

Deep raised beds made from galvanized water tank (bottom cut off)

Compost

Each bed has a variety of vegetables growing in it

Manure

Drainage rubble

Handy temporary space for seedling trays

Dumpy bag

Corrugated iron

A small, enclosed garden that uses every last bit of space to best effect.

A garden made entirely from recycled and salvaged materials – lots of time and effort, but almost no cost.

HOW TO MAKE A SMALL NO-DIG GARDEN

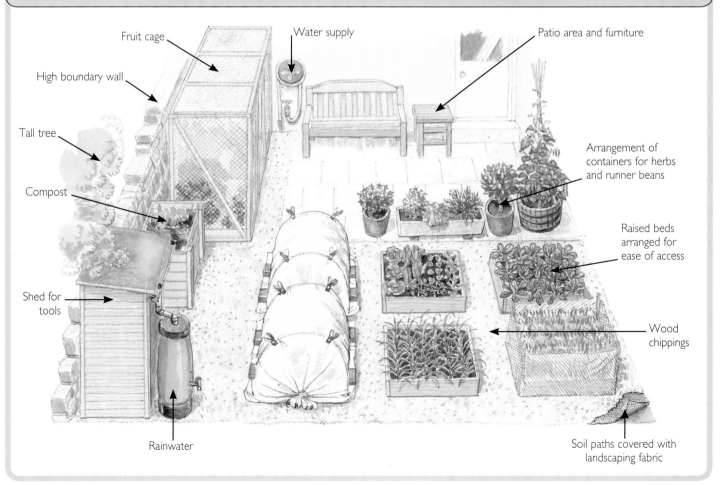

Fruit cage

Water supply

Patio area and furniture

High boundary wall

Tall tree

Arrangement of containers for herbs and runner beans

Compost

Raised beds arranged for ease of access

Shed for tools

Wood chippings

Rainwater

Soil paths covered with landscaping fabric

Raised bed construction

Are raised beds necessary?

Raised beds are an essential element of no-dig gardening. They contain and define the growing area and allow you swiftly to create an ideal growing medium. The decomposing layers of various organic materials within the bed mirror nature and reduce the need for watering and weeding. The width of the bed means that you can work without compacting the growing area, and the height of the bed can be adjusted.

RAISED BEDS FROM FOUND ITEMS

An attractive raised bed made from an old cast-iron bath.

A raised bed made from a builders' dumpy bag is good for runner beans.

Raised beds can be created from various materials ranging from old bricks and salvaged timber through to found containers such as tin baths, dustbins, wooden boats, wheelbarrows, water tanks, apple orchard bins and builders' 'dumpy' or 'jumbo' bags (used for delivering sand and gravel). Containers that are at least 60 cm (2 ft) in width or diameter are most useful. Old railway sleepers (large baulks of preserved timber) make excellent beds but are very heavy. Containers must allow for drainage – if there are no holes in the bottom, is it possible to make some? Thin metal containers offer less protection in frosty weather so are not ideal. Before using dumpy bags and pallets, check that they are non-returnable.

Making a raised bed from a dumpy bag

Step 1
Cut 2.5 cm (1 in) diameter plastic water pipe to length so that it makes a hoop that is a snug fit within the neck of your found dumpy bag

Step 5
Add more layers of compost and manure, and materials that will compost, until the bag bulges to clinch the hoop in place

Step 2
Trim a piece of found wood to size (so that it is a tight fit in the tube) and use it to link the two ends of the pipe to make a hoop

Step 4
Put the hoop over the outside of the bag and fold the top of the bag over-and-out so that the hoop is contained. Use a bodkin and nylon yarn to oversew the neck of the bag so that the hoop stays put

Step 3
Sit the dumpy bag on the ground, or better still on a found wooden pallet, and half-fill it with layers of manure and organic materials that will compost

BUILDING A RAISED BED USING TREATED WOOD

• The optimum width of a bed is around 90 cm (3 ft) – any wider and it is difficult to reach across (you need to avoid walking on the growing medium); any narrower and it will result in a less efficient use of materials. It can be square (as shown in the sequence below) or a rectangular shape (as long as you like), but always consider the site and your specific requirements (see pages 8–11).

• Frames assembled acording to the design below can be stacked one upon another, so that the overall depth can be adjusted for specific crops.

• Timber treated with preservative will make a long-lasting structure (lasting up to 20 years). It is worth using stainless-steel screws to avoid rust problems.

1 *You will need: four planks that are 23 cm (9 in) wide, 5 cm (2 in) thick and 90 cm (3 ft) long; and four posts that are 23 cm (9 in) long and 7.5 cm (3 in) square.*

2 *Screw a post to the end of a plank as shown above so that it is aligned to the end but offset by 2.5 cm (1 in). The protruding post facilitates stacking. Repeat for the other planks and posts.*

3 *Assemble the pieces to make a square frame.*

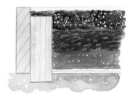

4 *Set the frame stub side down on the levelled ground, scrape off any weeds, and then fill it up in layers in the following order: newspaper and brown card, 5 cm (2 in) compost, 5 cm (2 in) farmyard manure, and 7.5 cm (3 in) spent mushroom compost.*

CONSIDERING THE LAYOUT

The arrangement of the beds must allow for paths that are wide enough for a wheelbarrow to be pushed along, and for locations that take best advantage of the sun.

A square grid layout with 90 cm (3 ft) square beds set 75 cm (30 in) apart.

A long grid layout with beds 90 cm (3 ft) wide and at various lengths to suit the plot.

A layout composed of a mix of purpose-made beds and salvaged containers.

PREPARING THE GROUND

Beds need to be positioned on fairly level ground. If your site is sloping, consider levelling areas for a terraced effect. Brick or stone-built beds will require foundations which are slightly larger than the beds themselves. Mark out areas using pegs, string and a large tape measure.

CONSTRUCTING THE PATHS AROUND THE BEDS

Paths are essential and can be constructed quickly using plastic sheet and wood chippings as shown below. The advantage of wood chip paths is that they are easily rebuilt or re-routed to accommodate any changes in layout that you may find necessary over time. Paths made from gravel, concrete, paving slabs or bricks are more permanent.

Cover the ground with weed-suppressing plastic sheet followed by a 5 cm (2 in) layer of wood chippings.

Alternatively, cover the ground with found materials such as old carpet and plastic sheet. Make holes in any plastic to allow for drainage.

BUILDING RAISED BEDS USING RAILWAY SLEEPERS

If you are looking to build a permanent no-dig raised bed garden that ticks all the form and function boxes – meaning the garden must be a joy to the eye as well as functionally sound – then building the beds from used railway sleepers is a good option. The sleepers are expensive, difficult to move, and tricky to joint and put together, and the whole task will require a lot of sweat and effort – it takes two strong people to lift a sleeper into place – but once the beds are built they will be there for a lifetime. The other bit of good news is that, while sleepers are undoubtedly heavy, the weight and

structure of the beds is such that they can be placed with little or no ground work. If you are keen to make the beds from railway sleepers, a good starting point is to look at the shape of your garden and take measurements. Note that the ideal bed needs to be about 90 cm (3 ft) wide – so that you can work the bed from both sides without standing on the growing medium – and then start phoning around for facts and figures. Once you know the type of sleepers – their age and dimensions, and how much they cost to be delivered – you can start drawing up designs.

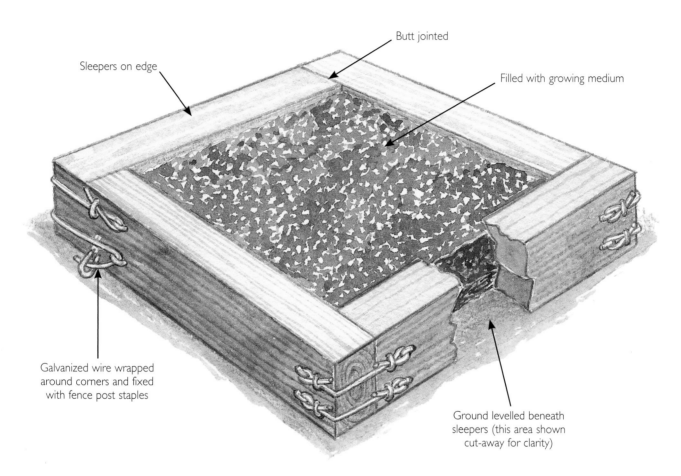

Butt jointed

Sleepers on edge

Filled with growing medium

Galvanized wire wrapped around corners and fixed with fence post staples

Ground levelled beneath sleepers (this area shown cut-away for clarity)

Designing bed modules

Salvaged railway sleepers measure 13–15 cm (5–6 in) in depth and 25–30 cm (10–12 in) in width. They come in a variety of lengths, from 1.8 m (6 ft) up to 4.3 m (14 ft). With sleepers weighing in at 45–110 kg (100–240 lb), they are difficult to cut and handle. It is vital to decide up front an overall module for the beds. Considering that the ideal bed width is 90 cm (3 ft), you need to measure the size of your plot, take into account that the paths need to be wide enough to take a wheelbarrow and then decide on a bed module size that makes the best use of sleeper lengths. You must do all this before you ever put tool to wood. A good way forward is to measure your plot, see what sleepers are available in your area, and then make a small working model.

Cutting

Salvaged railway sleepers are heavy, difficult to manhandle, and more often than not bristling with bent nails, rusty bolts, bits of wire and all sorts of foreign bodies, so you must always handle them with extreme care and caution – all the more so if you plan to use a chainsaw to cut them into lengths. There are three sawing options: you could cut them with a heavy-duty cross-cut handsaw, or with a chainsaw, or you could get them cut by the supplier. The important thing here is that the cuts must be true and square to the face and edge. If you have any doubts about your woodworking skills, then it is best to pay the extra and get the supplier to do the cutting. Make sure that you provide a precise cutting list.

RAISED BED LAYOUTS

A layout for a basic rectangular plot with a shed and a three-section compost bin.

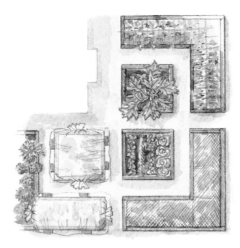

A layout for a difficult corner plot with house and garden walls to one side.

A layout for a corner plot where function is more important than decoration.

Maintaining beds and paths

- Beds made from railway sleepers and treated wood have a tendency to pull apart at the corners. A swift and easy repair is to clench the timbers together with sash clamps and bind the beds around with high-tensile heavy-duty fencing wire.

- Every two years scoop the rotted woodchip up off the paths, put it to one side to use on the beds as mulch and replace it with fresh.

- Avoid having a non-rot option on the paths, such as shingle, pea gravel or crushed shells, because, when the path eventually gets fouled up with growing medium, leaves and so on, they are difficult to wash.

- If you feel that some beds will later require a greater depth of growing medium to accommodate deep-rooted crops and/or crops that need to be earthed up as they grow, design the beds so that they can be built up with additional frames. (On page 13 we show how we have solved the extra height dilemma by developing a system of frames that notch together. This system could be modified to suit just about any bed material from brick to railway sleepers.)

- The depth of beds can be increased to suit gardeners who are in some way physically restricted, so that the gardener can work on a bed without bending or leaving the wheelchair.

JOINTING THE CORNERS

Railway sleepers can be positioned on edge or on face. For example a 15 x 25 cm (6 x 10 in) section sleeper can be positioned on edge to make a bed wall that is 15 cm (6 in) wide and 25 cm (10 in) high, or on face to make a wall 25 cm (10 in) wide and 15 cm (6 in) high. There are two basic options for jointing corners: they can be butt-jointed (cut straight through at right angles to the face and edge, and fitted end to side-end), or they can be cut at the ends to make simple half laps.

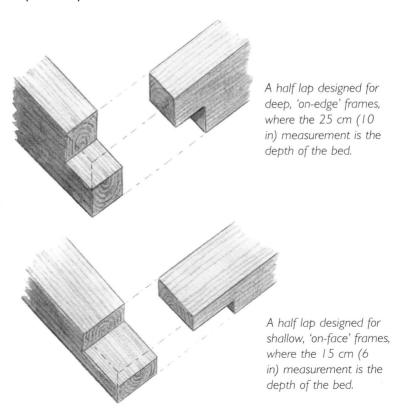

A half lap designed for deep, 'on-edge' frames, where the 25 cm (10 in) measurement is the depth of the bed.

A half lap designed for shallow, 'on-face' frames, where the 15 cm (6 in) measurement is the depth of the bed.

Growing medium

How important is the growing medium?

The quality and fertility of any growing medium is all-important, and in times past a keen gardener would spend a lifetime trying to improve their soil. The no-dig method sidesteps the slog involved by swiftly layering up manure, leafmould and compost to create the ideal medium. Once the basic mix of bought-in material is in place in the bed, you can top it up with mulches of organic manure and garden compost.

LEAFMOULD

Leafmould is a mix of fallen leaves from deciduous shrubs and trees that has been collected and encouraged to decompose rapidly. The leaves can be added in small amounts to existing compost bins, or stored in well-aerated purpose-made bins. Once decayed, the leafmould can be added to the raised beds as a mulch.

GARDEN COMPOST

Compost is a well-rotted mix of kitchen and garden plant waste – peelings and leftovers from the kitchen, and leaves and vegetable matter from the garden. A good option in the context of no-dig gardening is to have several compost heaps or bins on the go, so that leaves, stalks and general vegetable waste can be constantly recycled. While most weeds can be composted directly, weeds like thistles and nettles are best burnt – you can then use the resultant ash as a thin mulch or as a slug repellent.

SPENT MUSHROOM COMPOST

This is a waste product from mushroom farms that is relatively inexpensive, smells good, and is easy to handle. Never buy it by the bag, as it is far too expensive – it is much better to purchase it by the lorry load. It is a very good starter option when you are looking for bulk material to top up your first beds.

Leafmould

Garden compost

Spent mushroom compost

HOW TO MAKE A THREE-PART COMPOST BIN

A home-made compost bin is a good option, especially one like this three-part design. It is less expensive to make than three separate bins. In practice, while the first bin is being filled, the second has already been filled and is decomposing, and the third is full of compost that is ready to use. When the third bin is empty it becomes the first, and so on in a continuous cycle. Use reclaimed materials or buy treated timber and assemble using galvanized nails or screws.

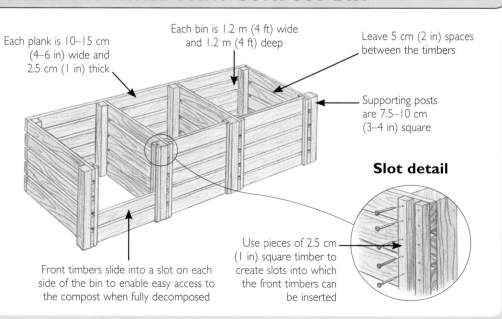

Each plank is 10–15 cm (4–6 in) wide and 2.5 cm (1 in) thick

Each bin is 1.2 m (4 ft) wide and 1.2 m (4 ft) deep

Leave 5 cm (2 in) spaces between the timbers

Supporting posts are 7.5–10 cm (3–4 in) square

Slot detail

Front timbers slide into a slot on each side of the bin to enable easy access to the compost when fully decomposed

Use pieces of 2.5 cm (1 in) square timber to create slots into which the front timbers can be inserted

Manure

Organic manure is the excrement from domesticated livestock such as cows, horses, poultry, pigs, goats, rabbits and sheep that have been fed on organically grown fodder. It usually comes as bedding, that is mixed with straw, chopped newspaper, sawdust or wood chips. Cow, horse and poultry manures are best, since they are stiff-textured, sweet-smelling, relatively free from harmful organisms, and readily available.

What is well-rotted organic manure?

TYPES OF ANIMAL MANURE

The only surefire way of ensuring that your manure is free from chemicals is to keep your own livestock.

Horse manure At about 0.6 per cent nitrogen, horse manure is easy to handle, low in cost, sweet-smelling and readily available from farms and stables.

Cow manure At about 0.4 per cent nitrogen, cow manure is a good option if it is mixed with lots of absorbent straw.

Chicken manure At about 1.8 per cent nitrogen, chicken manure can be a bit messy to handle; it is especially smelly when it is fresh and wet. The best method is to use poultry house bedding. Chickens are a good choice if you want to keep your own animals.

Goose manure At about 0.5 per cent nitrogen, goose manure is also a good option if you want to keep your own livestock. The main difficulty is that farmyard geese tend to spread their manure. It is advisable to cover their sleeping and watering area with straw or sawdust bedding, and then collect the bedding when it is in a mess.

Rabbit manure High in nitrogen, rabbit manure is very good if you can get enough of it; some gardeners reckon that it is the best ever. It is available as a mix of manure and sawdust, and is very convenient and easy to handle. It has a sweet, strong, nutty smell.

Sheep manure High in nutrients, sheep manure is a difficult option because, as the sheep live most of their lives outside, the manure has to be collected by hand. It is an inexpensive, easy-to-handle choice when mixed with straw or hay.

Points to note

- Some farms are awash with chemicals – so you do have to make sure that your manure comes from a good, reliable, accredited, organic source.

- Your chosen manure might contain a lot of harmful but naturally occurring organisms – so make sure that you always wash your hands after contact.

- Fresh manures are too rich and strong for most growing plants – so it is best to let them sit and rot before use.

Chinese geese like these will produce plenty of top-quality organic manure that is ideal for using in the no-dig system.

KEEPING CHICKENS AND USING THE MANURE

Chickens have long been the traditional choice of livestock for home-makers, keen gardeners and homesteaders. They will recycle most of your kitchen scraps, help keep rough grass and weeds down, eat lots of garden bugs and pests, and, best of all, give you eggs, meat and unlimited manure. The first step is to decide on your needs (do you want big fat birds, hardy birds, large white eggs, or some other feature?) and then pick the most suitable breed. Chickens can be fed on leftover kitchen scraps and garden greens, but they also need grit, to help with their digestion, and a ready supply of either organic meal or layers pellets.

For managing the manure, you need to house them in a large, walk-in, shed-type chicken house with plenty of floor space and a good wide door for wheelbarrow access. Cover the floor with a bedding of straw, chopped newspaper or sawdust. When the bedding is in a mess, you have chicken manure that can be wheelbarrowed out and either added to the compost heap or rotted down and sprinkled on the raised beds as a thin mulch.

Bed and plant rotation

Why is rotation necessary?

Different crops take different nutrients from the soil or growing medium. If, for example, you repeatedly plant brassicas in the same bed, the growing medium will become depleted in nitrogen and the plants will become sick. The traditional rule of thumb is that you have a three-year rotation – meaning that you grow, say, brassicas in year one, root vegetables in year two, legumes and salad leaves in year three, and then go back to brassicas in year four.

Permanent

The following crops are defined as 'permanent' in the sense that they can remain in or near the same bed for a number of years:

- *Globe artichoke*
- *Asparagus*
- *Bay*
- *Borage*
- *Chervil*
- *Chives*
- *Dill*

Brassicas (rotated)

Brassicas and other plants that enjoy the same soil conditions:

- *Broccoli*
- *Brussels sprouts*
- *Cabbages*
- *Cauliflowers*
- *Kale*
- *Kohl rabi*
- *Radishes*

Legumes and salad crops (rotated)

- *Broad beans*
- *French beans*
- *Runner beans*
- *Beet leaf*
- *Celeriac*
- *Endives*
- *Lettuces*
- *Onions and shallots*
- *Peas*

Root vegetables (rotated)

Root vegetables and other plants that enjoy the same conditions:

- *Beetroot*
- *Carrots*
- *Celery*
- *Chicory*
- *Leeks*
- *Parsnips*
- *Potatoes*
- *Salsify*
- *Spinach*
- *Swedes*
- *Sweetcorn*
- *Turnips*

YEAR I

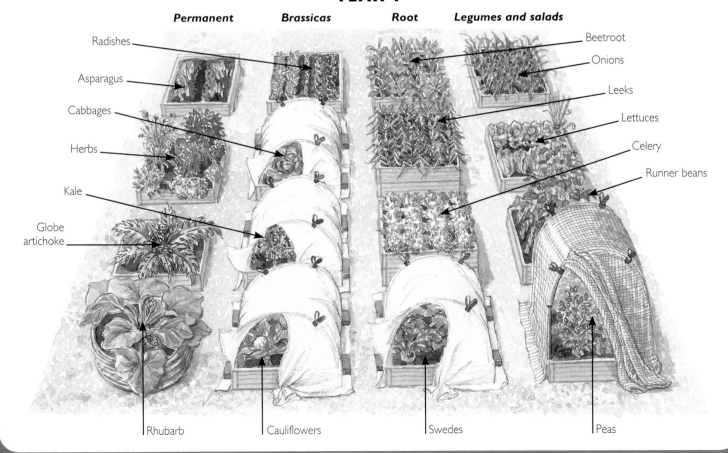

Permanent   Brassicas   Root   *Legumes and salads*

Radishes · Asparagus · Cabbages · Herbs · Kale · Globe artichoke · Beetroot · Onions · Leeks · Lettuces · Celery · Runner beans · Rhubarb · Cauliflowers · Swedes · Peas

YEAR 2

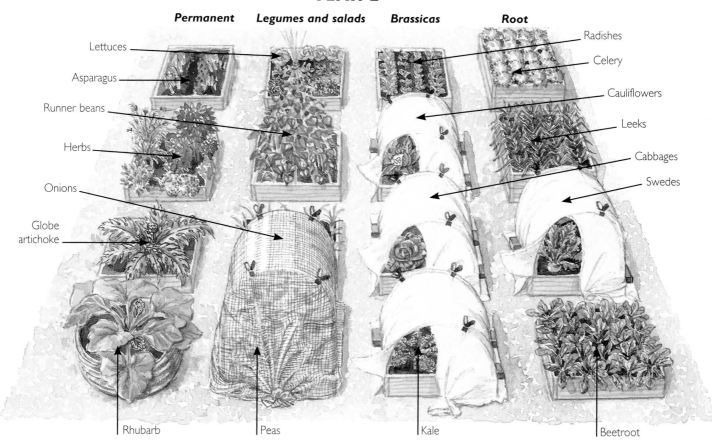

Permanent   Legumes and salads   Brassicas   Root

Lettuces
Asparagus
Runner beans
Herbs
Onions
Globe artichoke

Radishes
Celery
Cauliflowers
Leeks
Cabbages
Swedes

Rhubarb   Peas   Kale   Beetroot

YEAR 3

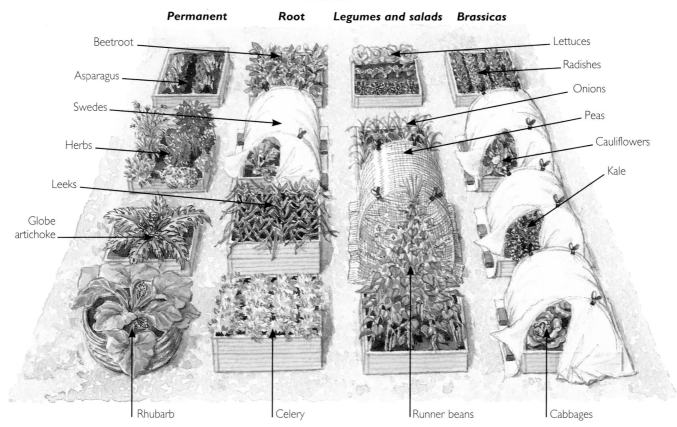

Permanent   Root   Legumes and salads   Brassicas

Beetroot
Asparagus
Swedes
Herbs
Leeks
Globe artichoke

Lettuces
Radishes
Onions
Peas
Cauliflowers
Kale

Rhubarb   Celery   Runner beans   Cabbages

Catch crops and intercropping

What is the difference?

Catch cropping and intercropping allow you to take full advantage of the growing potential of a bed. Catch cropping involves planting swift-growing vegetables in a vacant bed; intercropping involves planting swift-growing crops among slow-growing ones. For example, fast-growing salad leaves can be planted alongside celery, and radishes alongside beans. The disadvantage of both is that the closeness of the planting increases the risk of pests and diseases.

Swift-growing onions planted, or 'intercropped', each side of a row of slow-growing raspberries.

ARE THESE TECHNIQUES COMPLICATED?

While it is easy enough to plant a fast-growing crop in a vacant bed or between slow-growing plants, the complexity comes when the planting is so close that you have to monitor the beds constantly to ensure that the close-packed plants have enough light and air. It might seem a lot of fuss, but if you only have room for a small number of beds and you are prepared to put in the time and effort then it is no bad thing. That said, some plants seem to flourish when they are grown in a tight, companionable environment.

THE BENEFITS

The main benefit is that these methods allow you to swiftly take advantage of what you see happening on the ground. For example, if you see that a bed is empty or there is a lot of space between slow-growing crops, or a line of crops has failed, then you can swoop in and plant something that takes best advantage of the situation. The systems let you spontaneously make good use of what would otherwise be a 'lose-lose' situation.

COMPANION PLANTING

Companion, or beneficial, planting describes a situation where different types of plants are brought together for their mutual benefit. French marigolds and cabbages are a good example – the marigolds flourish while they protect the cabbages against whitefly by repelling the insects. Onions and carrots also work well together because the onions ward off carrot fly.

French marigolds can be grown alongside a range of crops to deter whitefly. They also look very pretty.

INTERCROPPING EXAMPLES

Broccoli and radishes

Step 1 MID-AUTUMN – plant Cos lettuce 30 cm (12 in) apart

Step 2 LATE WINTER TO EARLY SPRING – sow dwarf peas between alternate rows of lettuces

Step 4 EARLY TO MID-SUMMER – pick peas and plant broccoli 45 cm (18 in) apart; sow cabbage lettuces between the broccoli plants

Step 5 LATE SPRING – clear the ground, mulch with manure and plant pot-grown cucumbers

Step 6 LATE SUMMER – plant cauliflowers between the cucumbers

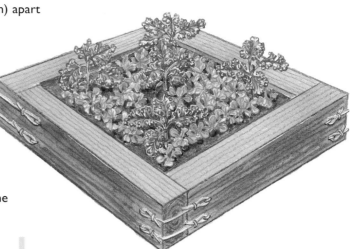

Cabbage and radishes

Step 1 EARLY SPRING – plant second early potatoes

Step 2 LATE SUMMER – lift potatoes and plant large and small varieties of cabbages 45 cm (18 in) apart

Step 3 MID-AUTUMN – plant cabbage lettuces 20 cm (8 in) apart in a row between the cabbages

Step 4 EARLY WINTER – lift the small cabbages

Step 5 LATE WINTER – clear the last of the small cabbages and plant broad beans in their place

Step 6 MID-SPRING – lift the last of the lettuces and sow a row of runner beans to fill the space

Step 7 MID-WINTER – lift all the beans, remulch and plant shallots

Step 8 EARLY SUMMER – lift all the shallots, mulch with manure and plant with celery 30 cm (12 in) apart; sow radishes between the rows

Parsnips and lettuces

Step 1 LATE WINTER – plant two rows of cabbage lettuces 30 cm (12 in) apart

Step 2 EARLY SPRING – plant cauliflowers between alternate lettuces; sow carrots between the two rows

Step 3 LATE SPRING – clear the lettuces and set pot-grown dwarf beans between the cauliflowers

Step 4 EARLY SUMMER – lift the cauliflowers, beans and carrots

Step 5 MID-SUMMER – plant celery in two trenches; plant spinach or lettuces between the celery plants; follow the celery with parsnips, carrots and beet

Organic protection

There is no need for chemicals in this system. To protect your crops, you can use mouse traps, physical barriers (such as nets, fleece, plastic sheet and wooden screens), beneficial insects and predatory bugs. Traditional home-made insect and disease controls are put together from ordinary household foods and products like garlic, vegetable oil and water. You can also purchase organic dusts and sprays, sprays made from milk, and washes made from water and soft soap.

GARDEN NETS

Depending upon the mesh size, configuration and set-up, a carefully chosen net will protect your plants from cabbage white butterflies that lay eggs that result in caterpillars, birds that chomp away at buds and foliage, small animals like mice, rats, rabbits and squirrels that dig up seeds and eat pods and fruits, bad weather such as severe frosts and lashing winds, and so on. For example, we protect our pea beds from mice and birds with barriers of fine net, mouse traps and little tin cans that tinkle in the wind, and our newly planted calabrese with fleece and nets to keep off birds and a sheet of corrugated iron to protect from the wind. Of course, many of these organic controls and barriers are a good deal less than beautiful – there is nothing pretty about a bent and rusty sheet of tin – but they work. If you can protect your plants with nets, old net curtains, sheets of tin or whatever you can find, without poisoning yourself and the environment, that is ideal. If it works for you, and is safe and non-toxic, then it has to be a good idea.

Builders' scaffold nets are very practical – they are strong, long-lasting and low-cost, and they will keep off a wide range of birds, animals and other pests.

A net-covered frame made from bamboo poles is ideal for tall-growing plants.

A draped net provides swift and easy protection in the early growing stages.

A frame built from iron fence pins and plastic water pipe can be used to support a net.

A tightly stretched net over a water pipe frame is good for protecting strawberries.

AGRICULTURAL FLEECE

Agriculture fleece is a non-woven fabric – think of a combination of fine fluffy gauze, a bed duvet, a super-thin sheet of cotton wool and extremely fine netting. Sold in a whole range of grades and thicknesses, agricultural fleece has rapidly transformed gardening practices. It can be used like a net, to keep away pests such as butterflies, slugs, snails, flea beetles, spiders and birds. It can protect plants by cocooning them, to keep heat in and cold out. It can be put down on the ground to warm the soil and control weeds. It is so light that it can be draped directly over plants, and it is so strong that it can be fixed up on a framework to create a sort of fleece polytunnel.

For seedlings and young plants, use sticks to provide just enough support to take the weight of the fleece.

When the plants are more mature, they should be strong enough to take the weight of the fleece themselves without the need for any other support.

PHYSICAL PEST DETERRENTS

Simple, old-fashioned, home-made pest deterrents include trailing cotton streamers to deter pigeons from eating greens, crushed eggshells, soot, animal hair and bits of trailed knitting wool to make things difficult for slugs, snails and cutworms, spinning compact discs to scare off birds and squirrels, tinkling tin cans to frighten off rabbits and foxes, and copper wire stapled around the top of beds to keep off slugs. There is no proof that these actually work, but they recycle products that would otherwise go to waste, they are fun to make and set up, and there are many folk tales and stories that vouch for their efficiency.

Old, unwanted compact discs are good for scaring off birds and squirrels, which do not like the movement and 'glitter'.

Sowing seeds

What is the best way of sowing seeds?

The best way really depends upon the type of seed, the time of year, the location, whether or not you are trying to achieve an early crop, and your experiences with the last sowing. For example, to avoid trouble with mice eating expensive pea seeds planted directly in the raised bed, you could plant the seeds in plastic gutters full of growing compost in the greenhouse, and then slide them into place in the beds when they are well rooted.

SOWING SEEDS IN RAISED NO-DIG BEDS

We used for the most part to sow seeds variously in shallow dibbed holes, V-section drills and trays, and then pinch out or plant out. However, the cost of seeds is now so high, the raised bed method so intensive and the end crop so valued, that we now sow either a single seed or tiny pinch of seeds – depending upon the size – in shallow dibbed holes or spaced in drills, then either carefully thin out to leave a single best plant at each station or lift and replant; or we sow in individual pots or peat pots in the greenhouse or polytunnel, and then plant out. This way of working keeps costs down, saves effort, advances the crop and generally results in better germination and better yield. We still sow some root crops in drills and some small low-cost seeds in trays.

Sowing seeds in pots ensures that the seedlings are well protected in the vulnerable initial stages.

Seeds to sow in dibbed holes in the bed

- Beans, runner (see page 47).
- Chicory (see page 34).
- Garlic (see page 52).
- Land cress and salad leaves (see page 32).
- Lettuces (see page 33).
- Parsnips (see page 55).
- Potatoes (see page 53).
- Spinach (see page 36).
- Swedes (see page 57).
- Turnips (see page 58).

Seeds to sow in pots or trays

- Aubergines (see page 65).
- Beans, runner (see page 47).
- Broccoli (see page 37).
- Brussel sprouts (see page 41).
- Capsicums (sweet peppers) (see page 66).
- Cauliflowers (see page 39).
- Celeriac (see page 61).
- Celery (see page 43).
- Cucumbers (see page 64).
- Kale (curly) (see page 40).
- Leeks (see page 51).
- Marrows and courgettes (see page 63).
- Onions (see page 50).
- Peas (see page 45).
- Sweetcorn (see page 49).
- Tomatoes (see page 62).

Seeds to sow into drills in the bed

- Beet leaf (see page 35).
- Beetroot (see page 56).
- Broccoli (see page 37).
- Brussel sprouts (see page 41).
- Cabbages (see page 38).
- Carrots (see page 54).
- Cauliflowers (see page 39).
- Kale (curly) (see page 40).
- Peas (see page 45).
- Radishes (see page 59).

TRAYS

1 *Cover the drainage holes with bits of broken crock, fill the tray with moist growing compost, and use a wooden board to press it down firmly.*

2 *Use your palm or a folded piece of paper and the gently tapping action of your fingertips to distribute the seeds gently.*

3 *Use a sieve to cover the seeds with a sprinkling of compost so that the depth of the layer suits the type of seed.*

SOWING IN THE GROUND

Potatoes	**Onions**	**Trench drill**	**V-section drill**

Dig a shallow hole and position the seed potato.

Make a shallow hole with a round-ended dibber and gently put the onion sets into place.

Make a wide shallow drill – a trench – and place each seed by hand.

Make a shallow V-section drill and dribble or trail the seed into it.

GUTTER

Cut plastic gutter to lengths to suit the width of your raised bed – say 90 cm (3 ft). Tape the ends up with plastic duct/gaffer tape. Fill the resulting long trays up with growing compost and sow your seeds as for trays. This option is especially good for sowing peas to stop them being eaten by mice. When the plants are well established, slide the plants with the growing medium into place in the prepared bed and water generously.

Potting on and planting out

Why are these stages necessary?

Some seeds, like those of courgettes, are sown in the greenhouse and then transplanted into the beds as seedlings, while others, like those of carrots, are often sown directly into the beds. Those that are sown under cover usually undergo various stages of 'potting on' – meaning they are moved into a slightly larger pot – before the young plants are strong enough to be planted out, or transplanted, into their permanent places in the raised bed.

Sowing seeds in 'cell' trays allows for much easier management of the seedlings when it is time to pot them on.

Delicate seedlings need to be transferred from seed trays and cells into larger pots to 'harden off' before being planted out.

Some medium-hardy plants, like these celery seedlings, can be planted directly out into the bed without being potted on.

Some plants, like these strawberries, can be propagated by pegging their 'runners' directly into pots, where new plants will form.

Potting on

When tray-sown seedlings are just large enough to handle, they are sometimes lifted, thinned out and transferred (this is also known as 'pricking off') into another tray or into pots, so that each seedling has more space and sometimes more depth of growing medium. Potting on can be fiddly and time-consuming, but this extra effort usually pays off in the quantity and quality of the resulting crop.

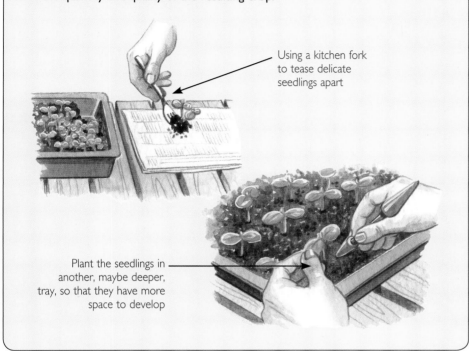

Using a kitchen fork to tease delicate seedlings apart

Plant the seedlings in another, maybe deeper, tray, so that they have more space to develop

Planting out

This is the end procedure of taking a seedling from a protected environment – the greenhouse, polytunnel, or covered bed – and putting it into its final place in the bed. Some crops, like celery, might have been sown in trays in the greenhouse, transplanted to a pot, and potted on to a larger pot or even a peat pot, all before being planted out in the bed.

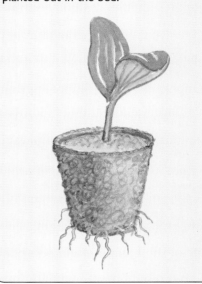

Thinning

This involves thinning out a mass of seedlings, such as might be found in a seed-tray in the greenhouse or a line in a seed bed – so that the spacing allows the plants to reach their potential. For example, you might sprinkle minute seeds like carrots in a V-section drill in a bed and then, when the little seedlings are big enough to handle, pull up and remove some seedlings so that the remaining seedlings have space to develop.

Remove the weak plants so that the best seedlings are left in place

Transplanting

Transplanting involves lifting fragile seedlings and setting them into their final growing space in the bed. Plants such as cabbages can be lifted by the trowel-full, teased apart and then transplanted. Plants such as tomatoes are best planted in pockets or peat pots so that the transplanting can be achieved with the minimum of root damage.

Always water the seedlings gently after transplanting

Extending the growing season

How can I maximize my crop yield?

You can easily extend the growing season by 6–8 weeks in your no-dig raised bed garden by sowing a few weeks earlier, say in a greenhouse or polytunnel, and finishing a few weeks later by protecting the growing plants with nets, fleece or clear plastic sheet. It is really worth considering this, as it will mean that you can enjoy your delicious home-grown produce over a much longer period for not much extra effort.

SOWING EARLIER

Looking at the recommended sowing times and temperature details on seed packets will show you that if you can increase local day and night temperatures by a just a few degrees – meaning temperature in and around the beds – and generally reduce the lowering of temperature by windchill effects, then it is possible to plant earlier. Just as our great-grandparents used cold frames, glass bell cloches, shields of calico and paper, straw mats and such devices for forcing, forwarding and protecting crops, you can use greenhouses, polytunnels, home-made shields, plastic nets and fleece to achieve the same effect.

HARVESTING LATER

Harvesting later is achieved by generally protecting the plants from the ravages of the weather. Of course, it is a bit tricky because once a plant's biological clock has started ticking there is a limit to how long you can extend its productive life. If, for example, you protect courgettes with fleece at the end of the season then it is possible to squeeze out an extra few weeks of courgettes on the plate.

These plastic cloches are good for getting strawberries off to a good start – they keep off pests and build up the heat.

Top ten methods

1 Cover the beds with fleece to keep out frosts.

2 Get off to an early start by growing crops in peat pots.

3 Start crops off in a greenhouse or polytunnel.

4 Stack extra frames on beds so that you can heap mulches up around tender plants.

5 Apply a mulch of straw to protect plants from frost.

6 Drape tent-like nets over beds to break gusty winds and draughts.

7 Put up screens to keep off winds.

8 Cover beds with chopped straw topped with old carpet to keep in the heat.

9 Surround a bed with a mound of fresh horse manure to create a warm environment.

10 Build a bed on a mound of fresh horse manure to raise the temperature of the bed.

A good-sized polytunnel will dramatically increase your yield, giving you an earlier start, a bigger crop and a longer season.

EXTENDING THE SEASON FEATURE EXAMPLES

Beans, runner

Normal season – sowing late spring; harvesting mid-summer through to early autumn.

No-dig raised bed season – sowing mid-spring in peat pots under glass for harvesting from mid-summer through to mid-autumn.

Tips
You can extend the season by starting extra early by planting the seeds in peat pots under glass and by saving the roots from the previous year; once the seedlings are in the beds you must use nets and fleece to protect them from late frosts.

Courgettes and marrows

Normal season – sowing mid-spring; harvesting mid-summer through to mid-autumn.

No-dig raised bed season – sowing mid-spring; harvesting mid-summer through to mid-autumn.

Tips
If you are prepared to create a bed on top of a deep-fill compost heap that has been well primed with a base of fresh horse manure, and to cover the bed with fleece the moment you have a frost warning, then you can bring sowing and planting out forward to the extent that you can advance the first cropping date by about two weeks.

Broccoli

Normal season – sowing mid-spring; harvesting early autumn through to mid-autumn.

No-dig raised bed season – sowing mid-to late spring; harvesting mid-winter to late spring and mid-summer through to late autumn.

Tips
By sowing early in a greenhouse, and sowing the full range of varieties – purple, white, perennial and calabrese – you can extend the cropping period so that you will be picking for about two four-month periods.

Beetroot

Normal season – sowing early spring; harvesting mid-summer through to late autumn.

No-dig raised bed season – sowing early spring; harvesting late spring through to late autumn.

Tips
The season is extended so that, by growing a full range of varieties and planting in succession, the first harvesting date merges with the last sowing.

Lettuces

Normal season – sowing late spring through to early autumn; harvesting early summer around to the following late spring.

No-dig raised bed season – sowing early spring through to mid-autumn; harvesting for the best part of a year.

Tips
To achieve a year-round supply, you must sow a whole range of varieties, always be ready with fleece, be vigilant with your watering, and sow in semi-hot frames in a polytunnel.

Celery

Normal season – sowing early spring; harvesting late summer around to late autumn.

No-dig raised bed season – early spring; harvesting late summer to late winter.

Tips
Sow early in the greenhouse.

Year-round calendar

The following calendar will not answer all your questions – because your growing medium and weather patterns will be specific to you and your area, and perhaps you will not want to plant all the vegetables on offer anyway – but it will at least give you some sort of timetable to work to.

MID-WINTER

Maintenance and preparation: Inspect your tools and sort out things like stakes, posts, string, pots, plastic sheets, netting and fleece. Set seed potatoes to sprout, order seeds, plan out the pattern of beds, and generally make ready.
Growing medium: Remove weeds, spread mulch, well-rotted manure or garden compost (as appropriate) and order seeds.
Sowing and planting: Plant broad beans in your chosen beds. Sow onions, leeks and radishes in a protected bed or hot bed.
Harvesting: Pick Brussels sprouts, winter cabbages, last of the carrots, celery, chicory and anything else that is ready.

LATE WINTER

Maintenance and preparation: Clean up the paths around the beds and generally make sure that all your gear is in good order. Cover beds at night with fleece and/or nets. Look at your master plan and see if you can get ahead with more mulching.
Growing medium: Use the hoe and rake to prepare seed beds – look for a nice warm corner and make sure that you have protective screens and fleece at the ready. Remove weeds; maybe add a thin mulch on selected beds, and put debris on the compost heap.
Sowing and planting: Plant artichokes and shallots. Sow early peas and maybe another row or two of broad beans. Sow carrots, lettuces and radishes under glass/plastic/mats on a hotbed. Raise seedlings of crops like leeks, cucumbers, onions and tomatoes in warm frames.
Harvesting: Pick Brussels sprouts, winter cabbages, last of the carrots, celery, chicory and anything else that is ready.

EARLY SPRING

Maintenance and preparation: Weed paths, mend frames and keep pulling up large weeds. Look at your plot and see if you want to change things around – perhaps the position of the permanent plot.
Growing medium: Keep stirring with the hoe and generally be on the lookout for weeds, especially deep-rooted perennials.
Sowing and planting: Sow hardy seeds such as lettuces and parsnips out of doors. Sow things like spinach, broccoli, leeks, onions, peas, celery, tomatoes and marrows under glass or in a protected bed – either directly in the bed or in trays.
Harvesting: Pick sprouts, cabbages and cauliflowers.

MID-SPRING

Maintenance and preparation: Be on the lookout for slugs and snails. Watch out for problems on fruit beds. Thin seedlings as necessary. Keep pulling up large weeds and putting down mulches. Reduce the number of sprouts on seed potatoes. Cover selected beds at night.
Growing medium: Keep working the beds with the hoe and your hands, along the rows of seedlings. Draw the soil up on potatoes.
Sowing and planting: You can now sow just about everything and anything in the open. Plant maincrop potatoes. Plant onions, radishes, maincrop carrots, beet, salsify and scorzonera, endives, more lettuces,

peas and spinach. Plant out any seedlings that you have hardened off, such as Brussels sprouts. Sow runner beans, marrows and courgettes under glass.
Harvesting: You can pick beet leaf and broccoli.

LATE SPRING

Maintenance and preparation: Keep a watch on the weather and be ready to protect tender seedlings with glass, plastic sheet, net screens or whatever seems to be appropriate. Be ready to deal with blackfly on beans. Set twigs among the peas. Put mulch on selected beds. Reduce the number of runners on the strawberries. Water seedlings. Keep on delicately hoeing and weeding.
Growing medium: Prepare more seed beds. Hoe and rake regularly. Heap up the growing medium to protect potatoes. Mulch between rows of more advanced vegetables.
Sowing and planting: Plant out hardy seedlings. Sow tender vegetables in vacant beds. Sow French, runner and brown beans in the open. Sow more peas, endives, radishes and summer spinach – almost anything that takes your fancy. Plant out Brussels sprouts, broccoli, cucumbers and anything else you like.
Harvesting: Pick beet leaf, broccoli, early beetroot, early carrots, cucumbers under cover, endives and many other vegetables.

EARLY SUMMER

Maintenance and preparation: Bring in fresh manure, well-rotted manure and spent mushroom compost. Keep everything well watered. Spread mulches around crops like turnips. Put nets over fruit. Remove weak canes from raspberries. Clean out empty beds and keep hoeing and weeding. Stake up runner beans and peas.
Growing medium: Keep hoeing. Dig up potatoes. Weed vacant seedbeds.
Sowing and planting: Plant out seedlings. Sow succession crops such as endives, lettuces and radishes.
Harvesting: Pick anything that takes your fancy.

MID-SUMMER

Maintenance and preparation: Support plants that look hot and droopy. Gather soft fruits as required. Cut mint and herbs ready for drying. Top-dress with manure mulch. Look at the tomatoes and pinch out and feed as necessary. Lift potatoes. Keep hoeing between crops. Water and weed. Make sure that any polytunnels, greenhouses and frames are open to the air.
Growing medium: Weed, hoe and mulch. Weed after lifting potatoes. Earth up maincrop potatoes.
Sowing and planting: Plant out the celery and crops like cabbages, sprouts and broccoli.
Harvesting: Just keep picking, eating and storing.

LATE SUMMER

Maintenance and preparation: Order seeds for autumn sowing. Keep storing vegetables for the winter by bottling, drying and freezing. Bend over the necks of onions. Dry herbs. Pinch out the tops of tomatoes. Clear and mulch beds. Protect fruit crops from the birds. Plant out new strawberry beds. Keep hoeing and weeding.

Growing medium: Weed and hoe. Weed empty potato beds.
Sowing and planting: Make more sowings of endives, radishes, spinach, onions and anything else that fits the season. Sow lettuces and salad crops under cover. Sow cabbages for spring planting.
Harvesting: Just keep picking, eating and storing. Dry more herbs. Gather beans, tomatoes, and fruit as and when they are ready.

EARLY AUTUMN

Maintenance and preparation: Watch out and protect from frosts. Lift and store roots. Earth up celery and leeks. Watch out and destroy caterpillars. Prune raspberries. Water, weed and hoe as necessary. Blanch endives.
Growing medium: Weed, hoe and mulch the moment you have cleared the crops.
Sowing and planting: Plant out spring cabbages. Look at your seed packets and sow if possible.
Harvesting: Lift potatoes and onions. Gather runner beans. Lift and store roots. Gather and store fruit as it ripens. Keep picking and eating other crops as required.

MID-AUTUMN

Maintenance and preparation: Watch out for frost and protect as needed. Mulch vacant beds. Continue hoeing and weeding. Clear the ground and put debris on the compost heap. Clean up paths and maintain beds. Thin onions.
Growing medium: Weed, hoe and mulch beds as they become vacant.
Sowing and planting: Plant rhubarb and fruit trees. Sow peas in a protected beds. Sow salad crops under glass. Plant out seedlings. Sow early peas in warm areas.
Harvesting: Gather the remaining tomatoes. Lift and pick crops like celeriac and carrots.

LATE AUTUMN

Maintenance and preparation: Watch out for frost and protect as needed. Clean up leaves and debris, and weed and mulch vacant beds. Continue hoeing and weeding as necessary. Remove bean and pea sticks and poles.
Growing medium: Weed, hoe and mulch beds as they become vacant.
Sowing and planting: Sow broad beans in a sheltered spot.
Harvesting: Lift and store root crops. Cut, lift and eat other crops as needed.

EARLY WINTER

Maintenance and preparation: Watch out for frosts and protect as needed. Clean tools and the shed.
Growing medium: Weed hoe and mulch beds as they become vacant. Check that stored vegetables are in good order.
Sowing and planting: If the weather is very mild, you could plant broad beans. Draw growing medium up around the peas. Sow salad crops under glass and protect as needed.
Harvesting: Pick the last of the beet leaf. Pick Brussels sprouts, winter cabbages, last of the carrots, celery, chicory and anything else that is ready.

Sowing table

The following quick-reference sowing table gives the sowing times and the ideal distances between plants for a wide variety of vegetables. Remember that the intensive no-dig method allows you to maximize the growing area by growing in a much tighter grid pattern.

QUICK-REFERENCE SOWING TABLE

CROP	SEWING TIME	DISTANCE APART
Artichokes, globe	sow mid-spring	45–90 cm (18–36 in) apart
Artichokes, Jerusalem	plant late winter to mid-spring	25 cm (10 in) apart
Asparagus	sow early to mid-spring	45 cm (18 in) apart
Aubergines	sow early spring	30–45 cm (12–18 in) apart
Beans, broad	sow late winter to mid-spring or late autumn	20–25 cm (8–10 in) apart
Beans, French	Sow mid-spring to early summer	13–15 cm (5–6 in) apart
Beans, runner	Sow late spring to early summer	15–20 cm (6–8 in) apart
Beet leaf	sow mid- to late spring	20–25 cm (8–10 in) apart
Beetroot	sow early spring to late summer	10–13 cm (4–5 in) apart
Broccoli	sow mid- to late spring	30–45 cm (12–18 in) apart
Brussels sprouts	sow early to mid-spring	45–90 cm (18–36 in) apart
Cabbages	sow spring varieties mid- to late summer, summer varieties late winter to late spring, winter varieties early to late spring	all 30 cm (12 in) apart
Capsicums (sweet peppers)	sow late winter to early spring	30–45 cm (12–18 in) apart
Carrots	sow early spring to early summer	5–7.5 cm (2–3 in) apart
Cauliflowers	sow early to late spring	30–45 cm (12–18 in) apart
Celeriac	sow early to mid-spring, plant out late spring to early summer	25 cm (10 in) apart
Celery	sow early to mid-spring under glass, plant out late spring to early summer	23–30 cm (9–12 in) apart
Chicory	sow late spring to mid-summer	20 cm (8 in) apart
Cucumbers (outdoor ridge)	sow mid- to late spring	plant out 45 cm (18 in) apart
Garlic	plant out autumn to early spring	15–25 cm (6–10 in) apart
Kale	sow mid- to late spring, plant out early to late summer	38–45 cm (15–18 in) apart
Land cress	for autumn to spring crop sow mid- to late summer, for summer crop sow spring to early summer	20–25 cm (8–10 in) apart
Leeks	sow mid- to late winter or early to mid-spring, plant out mid-summer	15–20 cm (6–8 in) apart
Lettuces	sow spring varieties late summer to mid-autumn, summer varieties early spring to mid-summer	20–35 cm (8–10 in) apart
Marrows and courgettes	sow mid- to late spring	plant out late spring to early summer one plant to a 90 cm (3 ft) square box
Onions	sow early spring to late summer	5–15 cm (2–6 in) apart
Parsnips	sow late winter to mid-spring	13–15 cm (5–6 in) apart
Peas	sow early spring to mid-summer	13–15 cm (5–6 in) apart
Radishes	sow mid-winter to early autumn	5–7.5 cm (1–2 in) apart
Spinach, summer	sow late winter to late summer	23–30 cm (9–12 in) apart
Spinach, winter	sow mid-summer to early autumn	15 cm (6 in) apart
Swedes	sow mid-spring to mid-summer	15–23 cm (6–9 in) apart
Sweetcorn	sow mid-spring in peat pots	plant out in late spring 30–40 cm (12–16 in) apart
Tomatoes, indoors	sow late winter to early spring	60 cm (2 ft) apart
Tomatoes, outdoors	sow early spring to late spring	45 cm (18 in) apart
Turnips	sow mid-spring to late summer	15–23 cm (6–9 in) apart

Land cress and other salad leaves

Land cress and other salad leaves, such as rocket, lamb's lettuce and curled cress, can be eaten as a salad, cooked like spinach, chopped to make a soup, or dribbled with olive oil and stuffed between two slices of fresh brown bread to make a giant cress-like sandwich.

SOW ▽   **HARVEST** ▽

mid winter	late winter	early spring	mid spring	late spring	early summer	mid summer	late summer	early autumn	mid autumn	late autumn	early winter	mid winter	late winter	early spring	mid spring	late spring	early summer	mid summer	late summer	early autumn	mid autumn	late autumn	early winter

ABOUT LAND CRESS AND SALAD LEAVES

- While land cress and most of the other salad leaves can be grown in less favourable, damp, part-shaded areas of the garden, they do best in a well-watered area that ranges from dappled sun through to part shade.
- Used as a cress and lettuce substitute, most salad leaves can be ready 6–8 weeks after planting.
- You can use them as a cut-and-come-again crop – the more young leaves you pick, the more young leaves you get.

GROWING MEDIUM

Select a bed in a medium shaded part of the garden (not too much shade nor too much sun), and layer up mulches of well-rotted manure, garden compost and spent mushroom compost. Aim to include at least a bucketful of well-rotted manure in a 90 cm (3 ft) square bed.

SOWING AND PLANTING

- For an autumn to spring crop, sow in mid- to late summer; for a summer crop, sow from early spring to early summer. Sow little pinches of seed 6 mm (¼ in) deep on a 15–20 cm (6–8 in) grid. Compact the bed and water with a fine spray.
- As soon as the seedlings are well established, pinch weak ones out to leave the best plant at each station.

Growing medium: Fertile and moisture-retentive
Situation: Part sun to part shade
Harvest: Pick regularly when leaves are 7.5–10 cm (3–4 in) long

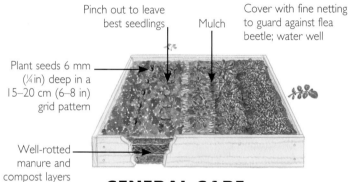

Pinch out to leave best seedlings

Mulch

Cover with fine netting to guard against flea beetle; water well

Plant seeds 6 mm (¼ in) deep in a 15–20 cm (6–8 in) grid pattern

Well-rotted manure and compost layers

GENERAL CARE

Stir the surface of the growing medium with a hoe to create a loose mulch, and hoe and water right through the season. If birds or insects are a nuisance, arrange a tent of fine netting over the whole bed. Remember that if the weather is hot and dry and you forget to pick or water, the plants will get ragged and maybe bolt. If some plants run to seed, the resulting seedlings can be planted on to fill gaps.

HARVESTING

You can harvest the winter crop from late autumn to early winter, and the summer crop from spring onwards – the precise time depends on your chosen varieties and growing methods. A good method is to go from plant to plant picking off the tender leaves when they are as long as your hand.

Troubleshooting

Slugs and snails The damage generally shows as holes and cuts in leaves. Remove the pests by hand on a daily basis.

Brown-edged leaves A sign that the plant is short of water, and/or you have neglected to pick the young tender leaves.

Flea beetle Hundreds of little holes appear in the leaves and there is general drooping of the plant. Avoid the problem next time by growing the plants under a shelter of fine horticultural netting.

Lettuces

Not long ago, we had crunchy Cos and soft butterhead lettuces, and that was it. Now we have leafy lettuce plants – round, soft, crisp, coloured and crinkly – to suit all tastes and seasons. Try different varieties, but remember to protect the beds if the weather turns too sunny or cold.

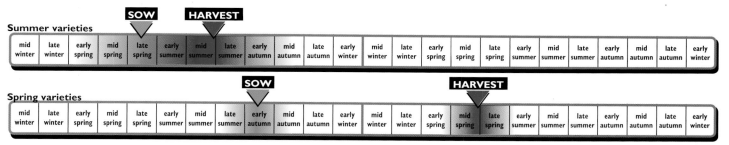

Summer varieties
(SOW above mid spring–late spring; HARVEST above mid summer)

mid winter	late winter	early spring	mid spring	late spring	early summer	mid summer	late summer	early autumn	mid autumn	late autumn	early winter	mid winter	late winter	early spring	mid spring	late spring	early summer	mid summer	late summer	early autumn	mid autumn	late autumn	early winter

Spring varieties
(SOW above early autumn; HARVEST above mid spring)

mid winter	late winter	early spring	mid spring	late spring	early summer	mid summer	late summer	early autumn	mid autumn	late autumn	early winter	mid winter	late winter	early spring	mid spring	late spring	early summer	mid summer	late summer	early autumn	mid autumn	late autumn	early winter

ABOUT LETTUCES

- Lettuces do best at a temperature of about 10–15°C (50–60°F) and need shade in very hot weather.
- You can grow lettuces intercropped with radishes.
- Butterhead varieties are sown in autumn for eating in spring. Crisphead or iceberg varieties are sown in late summer for eating in late autumn. Cos varieties are sown in autumn for eating in mid-winter through to mid-spring.

Growing medium: Light, fertile, moisture-retentive
Situation: Light shade in hot weather
Harvest: Cut when a firm heart is formed

GROWING MEDIUM

Lettuces thrive on a light, friable, moisture-retentive growing medium. There must be plenty of well-rotted manure and plenty of water in summer, and the underlying ground around the bed must be well drained. Layer the bed with mulches of garden compost, old well-rotted manure and spent mushroom compost, and be prepared to add sand or other material. Allow space around the bed for a shelter.

SOWING AND PLANTING

- Sow, according to the calendar above, a pinch of seeds 12 mm (½ in) deep on a 20–25 cm (8–10 in) grid pattern. Sow thinly, compact the growing medium and use a fine spray to water. Protect with glass or plastic. Vary the spacing according to variety.
- When the seedlings are well established, thin them out to leave one good plant at each station.

GENERAL CARE

Stir the surface of the growing medium with a hoe to create a loose mulch. Hoe and water through the season. Spread a net over the bed to protect from birds and pests. In hot, dry weather, water at least a couple of times a day. If the weather stays hot, spread a thin mulch of spent mushroom compost over the whole bed to retain moisture.

HARVESTING

When you harvest will depend on your chosen varieties and growing methods. As a general rule, if you offer the crop full protection you will be able to maximize your yield by sowing early and harvesting both early and late. Cut lettuces close to the ground as needed. Pick cut-and-come-again leafy varieties leaf by leaf – a few leaves from one plant and a few from another – until you have enough.

Troubleshooting

Slugs and snails Damage generally shows as holes and cuts in leaves. Remove the pests by hand on a daily basis.

Aphids Leaves are distorted with sticky colonies of greenfly. Spray with a water to wash off the sticky mess, scrape away 2.5 cm (1 in) or so of growing medium to remove the resulting mush, and burn all the remaining debris at the end of the season.

Brown-edged leaves These indicate that the plant is short of water. Avoid the problem by regular watering and by spreading extra mulch in long spells of hot, dry weather.

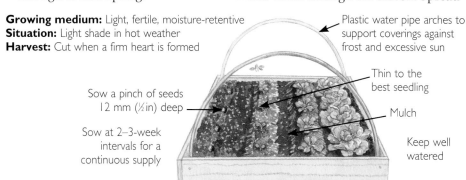

Sow a pinch of seeds 12 mm (½ in) deep

Sow at 2–3-week intervals for a continuous supply

Plastic water pipe arches to support coverings against frost and excessive sun

Thin to the best seedling

Mulch

Keep well watered

Chicory

If you take pleasure in sharp-tasting flavours and lots of crisp and crunchy bite in your winter salad sandwiches, if you have a greenhouse or cold frame and the use of a shed, and if you do not mind waiting a good part of the year before you get a crop, chicory is a good crop to choose.

					SOW							**HARVEST**												
mid winter	late winter	early spring	mid spring	late spring	early summer	mid summer	late summer	early autumn	mid autumn	late autumn	early winter	mid winter	late winter	early spring	mid spring	late spring	early summer	mid summer	late summer	early autumn	mid autumn	late autumn	early winter

ABOUT CHICORY

- A challenging but fun aspect of growing chicory is the way in which you can take the stored roots three or four at a time, from late autumn to early spring, and grow them up as fat buds or chicons.
- The self-blanching, lettuce-like chicory varieties are often easier to grow, but are somewhat lacking in taste and bite.
- The tangy, smoky, burnt taste of chicory nicely offsets sweeter foods such as bread, butter, beetroot and fish. Chicory is perfect in a fat brown-bread sandwich.

GROWING MEDIUM

The growing medium needs to be soft in texture, rich in well-rotted compost, fertile and moist. Be aware that a freshly manured bed will cause the roots of the growing chicory to divide. A good option is to spread plenty of manure for one crop and then follow on with the chicory. A handful of the growing medium should feel crumbly yet moist, but not so moist that there are sticky lumps. Choose a sunny corner, well away from draughts.

SOWING AND PLANTING

- **Late spring to mid-summer** Sow a pinch of seeds 12 mm (½ in) deep about 20 cm (8 in) apart, compact the growing medium, and water with a fine sprinkler.
- Thin the seedlings to the best plants.

GENERAL CARE

Water on a daily basis. Stir the surface of the growing medium with a hoe to create a loose mulch. Nurture the

plants through their growing cycle. At the end of the growing season, lift and trim off the leaves to about 2.5 cm (1 in) of the parsnip-like roots, and bed them, head to tail, flat in a box of dry sand.

HARVESTING

You can harvest and eat self-blanching varieties from mid-autumn to mid-winter. Blanch traditional types from mid- to late autumn through to mid-spring. To do this, take four roots at a time (ones that you stored in mid- to late autumn), plant them in a large pot in moist potting compost, cover the pot with black plastic sheet and put them in a medium-warm shed. They will be ready for eating in around 3–4 weeks.

Growing medium: Well-rotted compost, moist
Situation (not the chicons): Sheltered and sunny
Harvest: Cut with a sharp knife at the base

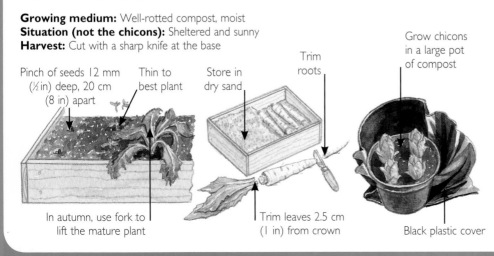

Pinch of seeds 12 mm (½ in) deep, 20 cm (8 in) apart

Thin to best plant

Store in dry sand

Trim roots

In autumn, use fork to lift the mature plant

Trim leaves 2.5 cm (1 in) from crown

Grow chicons in a large pot of compost

Black plastic cover

Troubleshooting

Leaf and stem damage Probably caused by a mix of slugs and cutworms. Hoe the ground around the plants, search out the pests and remove them.

Slugs Use slug barriers or traps and/or remove the slugs by hand.

Heart rot This shows as yellowy-brown damage to the leaves, and can be caused by frost damage or a virus. Avoid the problem next time by using frost- and virus-resistant varieties.

Beet leaf

All the difficulties of getting a continuous supply of spinach can easily be solved by growing beet leaf, also known as spinach beet, perpetual spinach and chard. It has a much stronger flavour than spinach, and the texture has a little more bite, but it is generally easier to grow.

SOW			HARVEST																				
mid winter	late winter	early spring	mid spring	late spring	early summer	mid summer	late summer	early autumn	mid autumn	late autumn	early winter	mid winter	late winter	early spring	mid spring	late spring	early summer	mid summer	late summer	early autumn	mid autumn	late autumn	early winter

ABOUT BEET LEAF

- Beet leaf is a good option if you are having trouble growing spinach.
- If you pick when young and tender, you can eat both the leaves and the colourful stalks.
- Late-sown roots can be lifted and grown on in the polytunnel for winter use.
- The coloured-stemmed varieties look good in the flower borders.
- If you grow the whole range of spinach and leaf beet varieties, you can be cropping all year round.

GROWING MEDIUM

Beet leaf does best in a well-manured bed in a sunny position, with the growing medium being moist but well drained. Although the plants are moderately hardy, to the extent that they can take a few degrees of frost, they will do really well if you lift and grow them in a polytunnel (see page 7), or if you protect the beds with nets or screens.

SOWING AND PLANTING

- **Mid- to late spring** Sow a pinch of 3–4 seeds about 18 mm (¾ in) deep at 23 cm (9 in) intervals across and along the bed. Compact the growing medium and water generously with a fine spray.
- When the seedlings are big enough to handle, pinch out to leave the strongest plants.

GENERAL CARE

If the weather is overly dry, and/or the plants look tired and worse for wear, firm up the growing medium around the

Growing medium: Well-manured
Situation: Sunny
Harvest: Cut stalks at the base with a sharp knife

plants and add an extra mulch of spent mushroom compost to restrict weed growth and hold in the moisture. Water generously in dry spells. Keep the plants in good order by removing flowers and old and yellow leaves.

HARVESTING

You can harvest from mid-summer round to the following summer – the time depends on the variety, where you live and how much protection you give the plants. Pick little and often to ensure a steady supply of young and tender leaves.

> ### Troubleshooting
>
> **Bolting** This is caused by lack of water. You can solve the problem by frequent mulching and daily watering.
>
> **Tough leaves and stalks** Prevent these by picking the leaves as soon as they are 15–20 cm (6–8 in) high. Give unwanted produce to neighbours or to your livestock, add it to the compost heap or sell it.

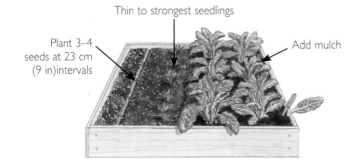

Thin to strongest seedlings

Plant 3–4 seeds at 23 cm (9 in) intervals

Add mulch

Spinach

When it is freshly picked, swiftly steamed and carefully drained, spinach is mouthwateringly delicious. There are alternatives to spinach, however, such as perpetual spinach, Swiss chard and New Zealand spinach, that might be better suited to your area.

			SOW							HARVEST														
mid winter	late winter	early spring	mid spring	late spring	early summer	mid summer	late summer	early autumn	mid autumn	late autumn	early winter	mid winter	late winter	early spring	mid spring	late spring	early summer	mid summer	late summer	early autumn	mid autumn	late autumn	early winter

ABOUT SPINACH

- As with a lot of vegetables, most people only get to eat the tired and much-travelled shop-bought variety and do not know about the succulent taste of fresh, home-grown spinach.
- Popeye the cartoon character loved spinach – it made him instantly strong and bursting with iron-fuelled energy.

GROWING MEDIUM

Spinach does well on almost any growing medium, so much so that it can be grown swiftly as a catch crop in the space between other vegetables. It does not matter too much if after a few pickings it bolts, because it can be swiftly resown at intervals through to late spring. While spinach will grow just about anywhere, it does best in a moisture-retentive bed that has been well manured for a previous crop.

SOWING AND PLANTING

- **Early spring to early summer** Sow a pinch of seeds in 2.5 cm (1 in) deep dibbed holes, about 7.5 cm (3 in) apart across the bed. Compact the growing medium and use a fine spray to water generously.
- When the seedlings are big enough to handle, first pinch out to leave the strongest plants 7.5 cm (3 in) apart, and

later remove every other plant to leave plants about 15 cm (6 in) apart. Water before and after thinning, and eat the thinnings.

GENERAL CARE

Stir the surface of the growing medium with a hoe to create a loose, moisture-retentive mulch. Water liberally. If the weather becomes dry, spread a generous layer of spent manure mulch between the plants, and keep watering. A shortage of water will bring about premature bolting.

HARVESTING

You can harvest for most of the year, depending on variety and growing methods. Pick the leaves by hand, breaking off old and tired leaves and removing debris as you do so.

Growing medium: Rich, moist and fertile
Situation: Sunny
Harvest: Use scissors to cut individual leaves

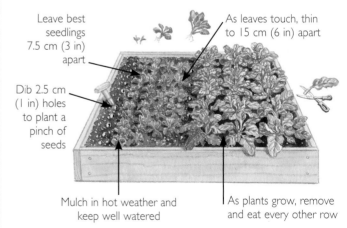

Leave best seedlings 7.5 cm (3 in) apart

As leaves touch, thin to 15 cm (6 in) apart

Dib 2.5 cm (1 in) holes to plant a pinch of seeds

Mulch in hot weather and keep well watered

As plants grow, remove and eat every other row

Troubleshooting

Distorted leaves Probably caused by spinach blight, a disease spread by aphids. Wash the aphids off with a liquid soap and water solution, pull up and burn badly affected plants, and avoid the problem next time by planting resistant varieties on a fresh bed.

Mouldy leaves These are likely to be the result of some sort of mildew. Avoid the problem by generous spacing, so that there is plenty of airflow between the plants.

Broccoli

Sprouting broccoli, both white and purple, is great when picked young. If you are really keen, are prepared to sow successive varieties and take care at every stage, you can, with a break in early summer, be eating broccoli – spears and flowers – from summer through to mid-autumn.

Calendar markers: **SOW** (above mid spring) | **PLANT** (above early summer) | **HARVEST** (Depends on variety, above early spring) **HARVEST** (above early autumn)

mid winter	late winter	early spring	mid spring	late spring	early summer	mid summer	late summer	early autumn	mid autumn	late autumn	early winter	mid winter	late winter	early spring	mid spring	late spring	early summer	mid summer	late summer	early autumn	mid autumn	late autumn	early winter

ABOUT BROCCOLI

- If you only know about tough and stringy shop-bought broccoli (the sort that looks good to the eye but leaves a bad fibrous feel in the mouth), home-grown broccoli is going to be a tasty, sweet and tender treat.
- Once the spears show, you can lengthen the cropping time by picking early at the shooting stage and picking late when the little flowers appear.
- The late flowers can be eaten in their own right and are very tasty.

GROWING MEDIUM

Broccoli does best on a heavy to fertile medium that is well manured and compact. A well-manured, moist but well-drained compact medium usually produces tight, compact flowerheads, while a loose, over-rich medium gives loose, open heads. Ideally, the bed needs to be sited in a spot that is open and sunny, yet not windy.

SOWING AND PLANTING

- **Mid- to late spring** Sow seeds about 6 mm (¼ in) deep in prepared seed beds or in deep seed-trays.
- **Early to mid-summer** Plant out on a dull and rainy day, so that you do not have to water, and so that the tender seedlings are not baked by the hot sun. Dib a grid of holes 30–45 cm (12–18 in) apart, and use lots of water to 'puddle' the seedlings into place – the spacing depends on variety. Use your fingers to compact the growing medium around the plants.
- You can also sow seeds in early summer for eating in late autumn.

Growing medium: Heavy and fertile
Situation: Open and sunny

GENERAL CARE

Water the seedlings before and after planting, and then daily. Stir the surface growing medium with a hoe to create a loose mulch and to keep it clean; add an extra mulch if the weather turns dry. Add another thin mulch of well-rotted compost when the plants are well established.

HARVESTING

You can harvest from mid-winter to late spring, and mid-summer to late autumn, depending on the variety and how much protection you give the plants (whether you grow in a polytunnel or cover with nets and fleece). Start by picking the central spear or head, and follow by picking the little sideshoots. Pick every few days to encourage new growth.

Troubleshooting

Caterpillars, butterflies and pigeons Cover the bed with netting to keep off most of the white butterflies and the pigeons, and remove caterpillars by hand. Inspect the plants daily.

Distorted leaves These can be caused by aphids and whitefly. Spray the plants with a solution of water and liquid soap. Remove damaged leaves.

Netting protection Make sure that you wash the netting at the start of the season, so that you remove potentially harmful insects and moulds.

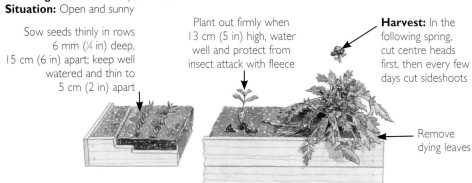

Sow seeds thinly in rows 6 mm (¼ in) deep, 15 cm (6 in) apart; keep well watered and thin to 5 cm (2 in) apart

Plant out firmly when 13 cm (5 in) high, water well and protect from insect attack with fleece

Harvest: In the following spring, cut centre heads first, then every few days cut sideshoots

Remove dying leaves

Cabbages

Cabbages are one of the most important vegetables because they provide a year-round supply of green food. They are easy to grow and come in all manner of exciting sizes, shapes, colours and textures – big as a football, pointed, crinkly, smooth, red, white and pink.

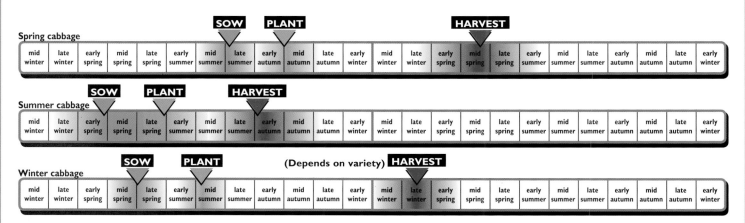

Spring cabbage — SOW (mid summer), PLANT (early autumn), HARVEST (mid spring)

mid winter	late winter	early spring	mid spring	late spring	early summer	mid summer	late summer	early autumn	mid autumn	late autumn	early winter	mid winter	late winter	early spring	mid spring	late spring	early summer	mid summer	late summer	early autumn	mid autumn	late autumn	early winter

Summer cabbage — SOW (late winter), PLANT (mid spring), HARVEST (early summer)

mid winter	late winter	early spring	mid spring	late spring	early summer	mid summer	late summer	early autumn	mid autumn	late autumn	early winter	mid winter	late winter	early spring	mid spring	late spring	early summer	mid summer	late summer	early autumn	mid autumn	late autumn	early winter

Winter cabbage — SOW (early spring), PLANT (late spring), (Depends on variety) HARVEST (late winter)

mid winter	late winter	early spring	mid spring	late spring	early summer	mid summer	late summer	early autumn	mid autumn	late autumn	early winter	mid winter	late winter	early spring	mid spring	late spring	early summer	mid summer	late summer	early autumn	mid autumn	late autumn	early winter

ABOUT CABBAGES

- With planning, you can be eating cabbages all year round.
- Cabbages easily fall victim to too much rain, too much sun, stiff frost, gusty winds, egg-laying butterflies, caterpillars, pigeons and slugs, so you will need to protect the plants.

GROWING MEDIUM

Cabbages thrive on a rich, firm, well-manured, well-drained, moist bed on a sheltered, wind-free site. Varieties like red cabbage require similar conditions, the only difference being that the growing medium needs to be richer.

SOWING AND PLANTING

- Sow seeds, according to the calendar above, 6 mm (¼ in) deep in prepared seed beds or deep seed-trays.
- Plant out according to the calendar above. Dib holes about 30 cm (1 ft) apart, to make a grid, and 'puddle' the seedlings in. Firm the growing medium up around the plants.

GENERAL CARE

Water the young plants daily. Use the hoe to pull the growing medium up around the plants to give protection against frost and wind. Once a week, in dry weather, stir the surface of the ground with a hoe to create a loose, water-holding mulch and to keep it free from weeds. Protect against pests by covering the plants with fleece, nets, or clear plastic screens.

HARVESTING

Harvest according to the calendar above. If you cut the cabbage off close to ground level and slash a deep 'X' on the end of the stump, four secondary mini-cabbages will sprout up.

Troubleshooting

Root fly Causes rotting stumps and blotchy foliage. Place a felt, plastic or carpet collar around the plant.

Leafmould This can seriously stunt the growth of the crop and future crops. Spray the spotted plants with an organic anti-mould mix.

Aphids Spray with a water and soap solution, wash the mess off with clean water, burn the top 2.5 cm (1 in) or so of growing medium, and burn the plants at the end of the season.

Holes in leaves Caused by caterpillars and birds. Avoid the problem by growing in a netted cage, like soft fruit.

Distorted roots and poor growth Probably caused by clubroot. Pull up and burn the plants, and rotate crops in the following year.

Rotting leaves A smelly, grey-brown rot caused by frost. Pull up and burn affected plants.

Growing medium: Manured, well-drained and firm
Situation: Open and sunny
Harvest: Cut stalk at the base with a sharp knife

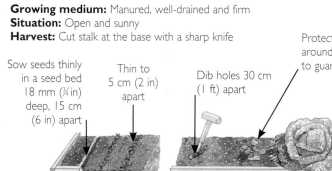

Sow seeds thinly in a seed bed 18 mm (¾ in) deep, 15 cm (6 in) apart

Thin to 5 cm (2 in) apart

Dib holes 30 cm (1 ft) apart

Protect from root fly with a collar around the base; also cover with fleece to guard against caterpillar attack

Draw up the medium around the stems and remove dead leaves

Summer cabbage (vary spacing for larger varieties)

Cauliflowers

Growing cauliflowers can be something of a challenge, but if they are well grown they are a joy. They can be used in soup and other dishes, but are superb when broken into large florets, swiftly steamed and served up with a hunk of home-made brown bread and a wedge of Stilton.

SOW **PLANT** **HARVEST** About nine months of the year depending on variety

mid winter	late winter	early spring	mid spring	late spring	early summer	mid summer	late summer	early autumn	mid autumn	late autumn	early winter	mid winter	late winter	early spring	mid spring	late spring	early summer	mid summer	late summer	early autumn	mid autumn	late autumn	early winter

ABOUT CAULIFLOWERS

- Although cauliflowers are easy to grow – meaning that it is simple enough to get a cauliflower with an averagely acceptable head – it is very difficult to get a really good, large, firm-headed specimen.
- Cauliflowers are very sensitive to any sort of check – poor growing medium, too dry, too wet, too cold, for example. If they experience a bad time at any point, they will grow wan and loose-headed.

GROWING MEDIUM

Cauliflowers do best in a firm, well-manured, well-drained, moisture-retentive medium in a sunny location. The manure or organic matter should not be fresh, rank or sitting on the surface; rather it needs to be well rotted, positioned at a lower level and well topped with spent compost. A good method is to manure the bed for some other crop, and then to follow on with cauliflowers. If the growing medium is really poor and/or dry, it is best to give up the idea of cauliflowers and grow another crop, because while the plants will most definitely grow in poor conditions, in the sense that they will show plenty of green leaves, the heads will most likely come to nothing.

Growing medium: Well-rotted manure under compost
Situation: Sunny
Harvest: Use a sharp knife to cut at the base

SOWING AND PLANTING

- **Early to late spring** Sow seeds about 12 mm (½ in) deep in well-prepared seed beds or seed-trays.
- **Early to mid-summer** Plant out in on a dull, rainy day, so that the young plants are not burned and dried by the hot sun. Dib holes about 30–45 cm (12–18 in) apart, so that there are no more than four plants in a 90 cm (3 ft) square bed. 'Puddle' the seedlings into the holes. Use your fingers to firm up the growing medium around the plants and water generously.
- Fit loose-fitting 'collars', cut from card, plastic or felt, to protect against root fly.

Note: Protect with fleece or fine net against caterpillar damage

GENERAL CARE

Water the seedlings before and after planting. Stir the surface of the growing medium with a hoe to create a loose mulch and to keep it clean, and spread a mulch of chopped straw or torn cardboard to further hold in the moisture. Water generously. As soon as a head shows, cover by gently folding one or more leaves over to keep it clean and to stop it yellowing.

HARVESTING

If you sow early, autumn and winter varieties, you can harvest from early to mid-summer and from early autumn to the following early summer. Cut the head complete with a few inner wrap-around leaves, or lift the whole plant and store in a frost-free shed.

Troubleshooting

Leaf spot This shows as rusty brown spots on the leaves. Do your best to get some sort of crop and then burn the rest of the plants at the end of the season, or simply cut your losses and burn the lot. Either way, use another bed next time.

Mealy aphids A sticky blue-grey mess of aphids is seen on the undersides of the leaves. Spray with a water and liquid soap solution to wash off the aphids, scrape up and remove the top 2.5 cm (1 in) of growing medium and burn the plants at the end of the season.

Holes in leaves Probably caused by caterpillars and/or birds. Prevent the problem by building a fine-net cage over the crop.

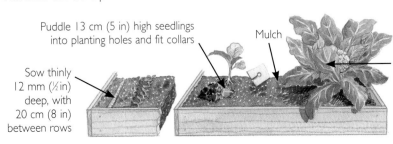

Puddle 13 cm (5 in) high seedlings into planting holes and fit collars

Mulch

Sow thinly 12 mm (½ in) deep, with 20 cm (8 in) between rows

When curds form, protect by snapping two large leaves as a cover

Kale

Kale, also known also as borecole and curly kale, is a somewhat forgotten vegetable. It is hardy, it can be cropped from late autumn to mid-spring, and the young leaves and shoots are so tender and tangy that they will set your taste buds tingling.

SOW	PLANT				HARVEST																			
mid winter	late winter	early spring	mid spring	late spring	early summer	mid summer	late summer	early autumn	mid autumn	late autumn	early winter	mid winter	late winter	early spring	mid spring	late spring	early summer	mid summer	late summer	early autumn	mid autumn	late autumn	early winter

ABOUT KALE

- Although kale is a good, dependable option in its own right, it is also a good choice when you are having problems with growing other greens – for example, if you have trouble with clubroot, heavy frosts or a poor growing medium.
- Kale can be cropped from mid-autumn right through winter to early spring.
- If your plot is very windy, which is not good for Brussels sprouts or large-headed cabbages, hardy low-growing varieties of kale are a good substitute.

GROWING MEDIUM

Kale does best on a strong, deeply worked, well-compacted fertile, growing medium in a sunny corner. It needs plenty of manure, but this must not be so rich and fresh that the plants roar away and become soft – all height and no breadth. A good method is to spread the manure for one crop and then follow on with the kale. In this way, the plants will start off slowly and become hardy. Although kale will put up with just about anything, it does not like loose ground, standing water, or standing water plus a long, hard, bitter frost.

SOWING AND PLANTING

- **Mid- to late spring** Sow seeds, about 12 mm (½ in) deep, directly in the prepared raised bed or in a seed-tray.
- **Early to late summer** Plant out, preferably on a dull, rainy day so that you do not have to follow on with the watering can. Lift the seedlings, dib holes 38–45 cm (15–18 in) apart in a grid across the bed, 'puddle' the seedlings into the holes and use your fingers to compact the growing medium around the plants. Water frequently over the next few days.

Growing medium: Deeply worked, compact and fertile
Situation: Sunny
Harvest: Removing young leaves with a sharp knife

When young, earth up to the base leaves

Remove dying leaves

Sow a pinch of seeds 12 mm (½ in) deep; thin to the best seedling

Woven wood screen for exposed situations

Protect with fleece from caterpillar attack

5 plants to 90 cm (3 ft) square bed

GENERAL CARE

Water daily. Stir the surface of the growing medium with a hoe to create a loose mulch, and draw the earth up around to give support and to protect from wind and frost. While kale will do OK on an exposed plot, if it is extra gusty you will need to build some sort of protective screen to the windward side – use close-mesh netting or perhaps a screen made from woven wood, not a plastic sheeting screen that will get blown away.

HARVESTING

You can harvest from late autumn to late spring. Use a knife to nip out the crown, and work down the plant picking off the sideshoots. Throw away all the old and yellow leaves and generally keep the surface of the bed free from any debris that might give shelter to slugs and other pests.

Troubleshooting

Mealy aphid This shows as lumpy-looking, blue-grey colonies of sticky aphids on the undersides of the leaves. Spray them off with a water and liquid soap solution, wash with clean water, scrap the top 2.5 cm (1 in) of the bed (to remove the mess of soap and insects), and follow through by burning the plants and all debris at the end of the season.

Poor growth, yellow leaves Probably caused by wind rock. Avoid the problem next time by supporting the plants with sticks, growing dwarf varieties, or choosing a bed that is well protected on the windward side.

Brussels sprouts

Sprouts are wonderful when lightly steamed and served up firm and tight with a dab of butter or a dash of olive oil, and disgusting when they are overcooked and presented as a soft, seaweedy sludge. If you and your family do not like sprouts, maybe you just need to modify your cooking skills!

		SOW			PLANT							HARVEST										
mid winter	late winter	early spring	mid spring	late spring	early summer	mid summer	late summer	early autumn	mid autumn	late autumn	early winter	mid winter	late winter	early spring	mid spring	late spring	early summer	mid summer	late summer	early autumn	mid autumn	late autumn	early winter

ABOUT BRUSSELS SPROUTS

- Some people seem to hate Brussels sprouts. This may be because shop-bought sprouts are not of the best quality, or because of the way they are usually cooked.
- Brussels like to be grown in a firm medium, with no rocking in the wind or shallow roots rattling about. They will grow in a loose, rich medium, and such plants will show huge amounts of foliage, but the actual sprouts on your plate will be loose, overblown and light in weight.

GROWING MEDIUM

Brussels sprouts do best in a firm, rich and fertile medium in a good-sized bed that allows for a long season of growth. They do not like to be packed into a small space, nor an overly windy site. A good option is to plant the sprouts in a bed that has been heavily manured for a preceding crop. The ideal is to have the bed in a sunny, open location that is protected from prevailing winds. If your area is windy, choose low-growing varieties and protect the plants with nets and/or woven screens.

SOWING AND PLANTING

- **Early to mid-spring** Sow seeds about 6 mm (¼ in) deep directly in a prepared seed bed or in deep seed-trays.
- **Late spring to early summer** Plant the seedlings out – this is best done on a dull rainy day, so that the plants are not baked in the hot sun. Firm the ground with your foot and dib holes 45–90 cm (18–36 in) apart, so that you have a staggered row with at least 45 cm (18 in) between plants. 'Puddle' the seedlings into the holes and use your fingers to compact the growing medium around the plants.

GENERAL CARE

Water the seedlings before and after planting, and then daily. Stir the surface of the medium with a hoe to create a loose mulch and to discourage weeds and troublesome insects. Take away the bottom leaves as they become yellow. When the plants are happily

established, spread a mulch of old spent manure or straw to further hold in the moisture. Firm up the growing medium in the autumn. Use strings, screens or nets to protect the growing plants from gusty winds.

HARVESTING

You can harvest from early autumn to early spring – the precise times depends on the variety and your growing methods. Work from bottom to top up the stem, picking only the best tight sprouts. Put tired and damaged sprouts and yellow leaves on the compost heap.

Growing medium: Fertile and firm
Situation: Sheltered and sunny
Harvest: Pick from the bottom before sprouts open

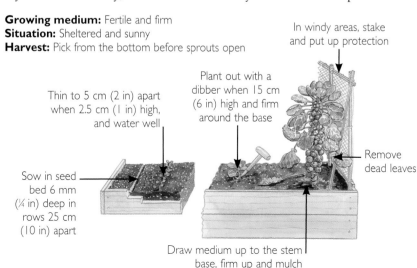

In windy areas, stake and put up protection

Plant out with a dibber when 15 cm (6 in) high and firm around the base

Remove dead leaves

Thin to 5 cm (2 in) apart when 2.5 cm (1 in) high, and water well

Sow in seed bed 6 mm (¼ in) deep in rows 25 cm (10 in) apart

Draw medium up to the stem base, firm up and mulch

Troubleshooting

Holes in leaves These are probably caused by caterpillars and/or birds. Avoid the problem by growing the sprouts in a netted cage like soft fruit.

Sticky distorted leaves These are most likely caused by aphids and whitefly. Remove badly damaged leaves, get rid of the mess by spraying with a solution of water and liquid soap, and then wash the plants with plenty of clean water. Scrape off the top 2.5 cm (1 in) or so of growing medium and put in on the bonfire.

Distorted root and poor growth Probably caused by clubroot. The best plan of action is to pull up and burn the plants, and plant all future brassicas at the other end of the garden.

Asparagus

Asparagus is now becoming a popular mainstream vegetable, although it was traditionally considered hard to grow. You might have to wait 3–4 years before you get a really good crop, but once the plants are well established you can expect them to crop for 20 years or more.

SOW PLANT

mid winter	late winter	early spring	mid spring	late spring	early summer	mid summer	late summer	early autumn	mid autumn	late autumn	early winter	mid winter	late winter	early spring	mid spring	late spring	early summer	mid summer	late summer	early autumn	mid autumn	late autumn	early winter

HARVEST

Year 2–3

mid winter	late winter	early spring	mid spring	late spring	early summer	mid summer	late summer	early autumn	mid autumn	late autumn	early winter	mid winter	late winter	early spring	mid spring	late spring	early summer	mid summer	late summer	early autumn	mid autumn	late autumn	early winter

ABOUT ASPARAGUS

- It is easier to grow from one-year-old crowns than seed.
- Some growers think that you can take a small crop in year two; others say that you should always hold back cropping into year three or even year four.

GROWING MEDIUM

Asparagus does best in a well-drained, deep, rich, slightly sandy medium that is layered up with a mix of well-rotted farmyard manure and spent mushroom compost. Choose a sheltered but sunny spot. Spread thin mulches of spent mushroom compost to keep down the weeds. You should have no more than one plant on a 90 cm (3 ft) square bed.

SOWING AND PLANTING

- **First year** Open up a trench about 25 cm (10 in) deep and 38 cm (15 in) wide. Cover the base with 7.5 cm (3 in) of gently mounded compost or well-rotted manure.
- **Early to mid-spring** Set the one-year-old crowns 45 cm (18 in) apart, with their roots spread over the mound, and cover with 5–7.5 cm (2–3 in) of well-rotted spent compost. Water generously.

GENERAL CARE

In the first year, let the plants grow until autumn. Just before the berries develop, cut away the foliage, clear away debris

and mulch with well-rotted manure topped with spent compost. Repeat in the second year. In the third year, in early spring draw the growing medium over the plants, in mid- to late spring cut selected spears, in summer leave the spears to grow and fall, and in late autumn clear debris and remulch.

HARVESTING

In the third season, from mid-spring to early summer, when good strong spears have pushed 7.5–10 cm (3–4 in) above ground, use your fingers to gently reveal the plant, and then, one spear at a time, take a long-bladed knife and slide the blade at a flat angle into the growing medium to cut the spear at a point 7.5–10 cm (3–4 in) below the ground.

Growing medium: Well-drained and fertile
Situation: Open and sunny

Harvest: 3rd year, sparingly; 4th year onwards, from late spring to early summer

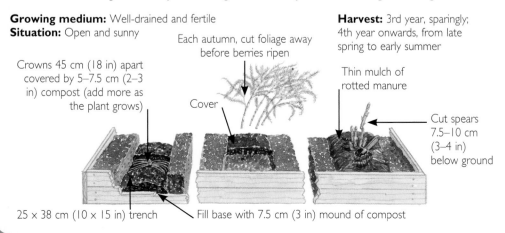

Crowns 45 cm (18 in) apart covered by 5–7.5 cm (2–3 in) compost (add more as the plant grows)

Each autumn, cut foliage away before berries ripen

Cover

Thin mulch of rotted manure

Cut spears 7.5–10 cm (3–4 in) below ground

25 x 38 cm (10 x 15 in) trench

Fill base with 7.5 cm (3 in) mound of compost

Troubleshooting

Slugs Use slug barriers or traps and/or remove the slugs by hand.

Roots dying Burn all the affected plants, and restart on a fresh bed.

Frost damage Cut away blackened shoots and protect from frost.

Poor cropping This is probably caused by cutting too much too early.

Celery

Growing celery is something of a challenge: digging trenches, binding the plants around with cardboard collars, earthing up, watering, more earthing up, and so on, but eating freshly picked celery through the winter months, in soups or with bread and cheese, makes it all worthwhile.

		SOW		**PLANT**						**HARVEST**															
mid winter	late winter	early spring	mid spring	late spring	early summer	mid summer	late summer	early autumn	mid autumn	late autumn	early winter	mid winter	late winter	early spring	mid spring	late spring	early summer	mid summer	late summer	early autumn	mid autumn	late autumn	early winter

ABOUT CELERY

- Growing celery involves lots of procedures and effort such as building extra frames, planting out, and stacking the frames for blanching. It is not particularly hard work, but it is time-consuming.
- Self-blanching varieties remove the need for earthing up, but many lack the taste and texture of the old forms.
- If you grow traditional and self-blanching varieties, you can be eating celery from mid-autumn to late winter.

GROWING MEDIUM

Celery does best in a deep, rich, heavy and moist but well-drained medium in an open and sunny position. The bed needs to be damp, but not so wet that water puddles on the surface – celery needs lots of water but will not do well if the bed is waterlogged or sour. Make sure that the bed is prepared well in advance with lots of well-rotted manure. The growing medium that you have drawn to the side in preparation for earthing up must be fine and friable.

SOWING AND PLANTING

- **Early to mid-spring** Sow seeds under glass about 12 mm (½ in) deep in prepared seed-trays. As soon as the seedlings are big enough to handle, pot them into peat pots.
- **Late spring to early summer** Plant out in a bed, 23 cm (9 in) apart.

GENERAL CARE

Water the plants daily. Stir the surface of the growing medium with a hoe to create a loose mulch. Remove suckers and debris. As the plants gain in height, add additional frames to the bed and keep topping up with mulches of well-rotted manure and garden compost so that the stalks are well covered. In frosty weather, cover the beds with a mulch of chopped straw or torn cardboard, followed by a thin mulch of spent mushroom compost topped with mats of card, carpet or anything that will keep out a stiff frost. Remove the mats if the weather turns wet or mild.

HARVESTING

Harvest self-blanching varieties from late summer to late autumn, and traditional varieties from late autumn to early spring. Use a fork to ease the plant from the ground. Leave remaining plants covered. At the end of the season, when the plants look finished, there is still a chance that the hearts can be saved after cutting away the squashy brown mess.

Growing medium: Deep, fertile and moist
Situation: Sunny
Harvest: Use a fork to lever it out

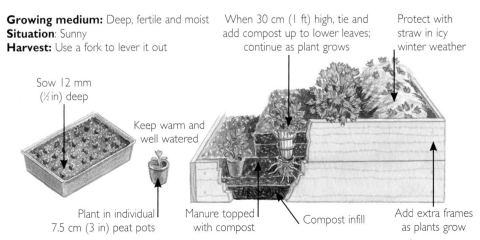

Sow 12 mm (½ in) deep

Keep warm and well watered

Plant in individual 7.5 cm (3 in) peat pots

Manure topped with compost

Compost infill

When 30 cm (1 ft) high, tie and add compost up to lower leaves; continue as plant grows

Add extra frames as plants grow

Protect with straw in icy winter weather

Troubleshooting

Brown spotted leaves Probably caused by viruses and/or fungi. Save what you can, pull up and burn the plants, and use a different bed next time.

Slugs and snails These create open wounds that can cause secondary damage. Remove them by hand on a daily basis.

Brown rot This shows as a rotten heart at the lifting stage. Burn the plants and try again on another plot.

Artichokes, globe

The exotic-looking globe artichoke is grown for its flowers, which form fleshy, scale-covered heads. Although it is a perennial that can be left in place in much the same way as rhubarb, it can just as easily be grown as an annual or even as a biennial.

				SOW	PLANT			HARVEST															
mid winter	late winter	early spring	mid spring	late spring	early summer	mid summer	late summer	early autumn	mid autumn	late autumn	early winter	mid winter	late winter	early spring	mid spring	late spring	early summer	mid summer	late summer	early autumn	mid autumn	late autumn	early winter

ABOUT GLOBE ARTICHOKES

- Globe artichokes can be grown from seed, or better still from root suckers, in much the same way as rhubarb.
- A healthy plant will grow to a height of about 1.2 m (4 ft).
- Throw away the first heads in the first year, and start cropping in earnest in the second season after planting.
- Plants reach their peak in the third or fourth year after planting.

GROWING MEDIUM

Traditionally it was grown in beds, in a deep, rich soil with full exposure to sunlight. It needs plenty of moisture throughout the summer months, and a well-drained growing medium during the winter. Prepare the bed with layers of well-rotted farmyard manure, with extra mulches of dung in the spring and autumn.

SOWING AND PLANTING

- **Mid-spring** Plant the suckers singly about 10 cm (4 in) deep, say two plants to a 90 cm (3 ft) square bed.
- Tread the plants in well, water daily and provide shade, until the plant looks to be well established.

Growing medium: Deep and rich
Situation: Sunny

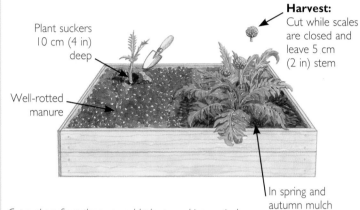

Plant suckers 10 cm (4 in) deep

Well-rotted manure

Harvest: Cut while scales are closed and leave 5 cm (2 in) stem

In spring and autumn mulch with dung

Cut suckers from three-year-old plants, making vertical knife cuts to separate a shoot with roots attached.

GENERAL CARE

In the first season, water and mulch, discard the heads in the winter, cut the foliage down to the ground and cover the crowns with straw. In the second season, remove the straw, and apply a mulch of manure in the spring. Huge heads can be tough and stringy, so go for the middle size.

HARVESTING

Harvest from early summer onwards when the heads are mature but the scales still closed. Cut the crowns off with 5–7.5 cm (2–3 in) of stem and stand them in water until needed. Cut the stems down and allow the new suckers to produce a late second crop.

Troubleshooting

Slugs Use slug barriers or traps and/or remove the slugs by hand.

Insect attack Pinch out affected areas, spray with a solution of water and liquid soap, remove the stale top 2.5 cm (1 in) of growing medium and replace with a fresh mulch of well-rotted manure.

Rust brown heads This is caused by fungus damage that affects the heads and flowers. Carefully cut and burn any affected plants.

Peas

Although botanically the pea is defined as a fruit, most people think of it as a vegetable. The fascinating thing is that although many children will make some sort of fuss about eating most other vegetables, they tend to like the taste, texture and shape of peas.

			SOW			**HARVEST**																	
mid winter	late winter	early spring	mid spring	late spring	early summer	mid summer	late summer	early autumn	mid autumn	late autumn	early winter	mid winter	late winter	early spring	mid spring	late spring	early summer	mid summer	late summer	early autumn	mid autumn	late autumn	early winter

ABOUT PEAS

- Peas take about 60 days to mature.
- Varieties like mangetout and sugar snap are eaten complete with their pods. Harvest when the peas just begin to show in the pods.

Growing medium: Well-drained and fertile
Situation: Sunny and sheltered
Harvest: Pick regularly before they toughen

- Pea roots store nitrogen, so bury them at the end of the season to improve the fertility of the growing medium.

GROWING MEDIUM

Peas do well in a deep, well-drained, moist growing medium that has been well manured for a previous crop, in a warm, sheltered position. Peas need lots of moisture. If you see that the bed is dry, soak it with water and mulch the bed with well-rotted spent manure.

SOWING AND PLANTING

- **Early spring to mid-summer** Sow seeds in 2.5–5 cm (1–2 in) deep drills in a 13–15 cm (5–6 in) grid across the bed, or under glass in lengths of 7.5 cm (3 in) wide plastic gutter; when the plants are established, slide them into place in the bed. Firm in and water generously.
- Cover the bed with wire mesh, twigs, cotton or fleece to keep the birds off.

- Watch out for pigeons, rabbits, mice and cats, which can all be a problem.

GENERAL CARE

When the plants are well established, stir the surface of the growing medium with a hoe. Repeat this at least every week, especially in dry weather. In long dry spells, drench the growing medium with water and heap a mulch of old manure over the bed. When the pods begin to fill out, cover the bed with nets and be on the lookout for mice.

HARVESTING

Harvest from early summer to mid-autumn. Peas swell rapidly, so gather them when young. Pick every 2–3 days to encourage new pods to develop.

Troubleshooting

Aphids These show as a sticky, grey mess on the underside of the foliage. Spray the mess off with a mix of water and liquid soap, wash with clean water, then scrape the resulting soapy mess up from the bed and burn it.

Mould and mildew This appears as yellow leaves and/or white patches, usually in dry weather. Drench with an organic spray; if this fails, save what you can of the crop, burn the plants, and choose a disease-resistant variety next time.

Mice A terribly frustrating nuisance. The best advice is to sow in the gutters as described above, and then make a huge effort to protect the growing plants with nets, fleece, wire mesh and traps.

Pea moth Little maggots are found within the pod. Eat what you can, and go for a different variety and a different bed next time.

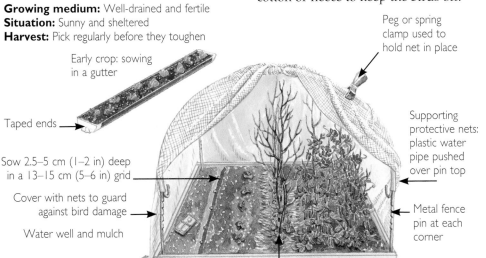

Early crop: sowing in a gutter

Taped ends

Sow 2.5–5 cm (1–2 in) deep in a 13–15 cm (5–6 in) grid

Cover with nets to guard against bird damage

Water well and mulch

Weigh down net bottom

Peg or spring clamp used to hold net in place

Supporting protective nets: plastic water pipe pushed over pin top

Metal fence pin at each corner

As tendrils develop, push pea sticks into the soil to support the plants

French beans

The flavour of French beans may not compare with runner beans, but they are well worth planting because they can be cropped two or three weeks before runner beans. If you plant them under cover, you can enjoy your first little bean feast early in the summer.

SOW **HARVEST**

mid winter	late winter	early spring	mid spring	late spring	early summer	mid summer	late summer	early autumn	mid autumn	late autumn	early winter	mid winter	late winter	early spring	mid spring	late spring	early summer	mid summer	late summer	early autumn	mid autumn	late autumn	early winter

FRENCH BEAN FACTS

- French beans like to be in an airy situation, to the extent that some varieties will present a splotchy leaf mildew if you overdo the fleece protection.
- French beans are a good option if you are short of space.
- You can lengthen the total season by planting a couple of weeks early and then by protecting the young plants with fleece and/or plastic netting.

GROWING MEDIUM

Although just about any well-prepared soil will yield a fair crop, French beans do best in a bed that has been generously mulched with well-rotted manure in the previous season. Dust the bed with a light dressing of lime a week or two before the seeds are sown. As soon as the plants are a few centimetres high, spread a mulch of old manure over the bed to hold in the moisture. Be aware, if you are planting extra early, that you must protect against gusty winds and draughts. As with runner beans, French beans must be protected against frosts and driving rain.

SOWING AND PLANTING

- **Mid- to late spring for early crop** Prepare 5 cm (2 in) deep drills. Sow the seeds about 15 cm (6 in) apart in all directions so that you get about 20 plants in a 90 cm (3 ft) square bed. Water generously.
- **Late spring through to early summer for main crop** Sow as above.
- **Early to late summer** Sow as above.
- Early and late crops will need to be protected with cloches, nets, mini polytunnels, or anything that keeps off the wind and frost.

GENERAL CARE

When the plants are a few centimetres high, very carefully draw the growing medium around the stems and, if the weather looks in any way cold or gusty, ring the bed with a screen of netting. When the plants look well established, spread a mulch of old spent manure or mushroom compost to hold back the weeds and to retain moisture. Water generously at the roots – but keep the water away from the foliage. Support climbing varieties. If the weather threatens to be windy, bind the bed of beans around with soft string, so that they give each other support, and rig up a screen on the windward side.

HARVESTING

You can start picking from mid-summer onwards when the pods are plump and firm. Pick with both hands, one hand supporting the stem and the other twisting off the pods.

Growing medium: Medium to light
Situation: Airy
Harvest: Pick regularly before they toughen

Seeds 5 cm (2 in) deep, 15 cm (6 in) apart

Pull earth up to support young plants

Old spent manure mulch

Troubleshooting

Blackfly Treat in the same way as broad beans.

Wilting stems Dispose of the plants and replant new ones.

Blotchy, brown-yellow leaves Likely to be blight. Dispose of damaged plants and avoid planting French beans on the same plot for a couple of years.

Runner beans

The runner bean is a wonderful and popular vegetable. Building the support structures is an inventive activity, and then the mature plants are pleasing to the eye, crop well and have a long growing season. A plate of runner beans sprinkled with olive oil and cider vinegar is quite delicious!

				SOW				**HARVEST**																
mid winter	late winter	early spring	mid spring	late spring	early summer	mid summer	late summer	early autumn	mid autumn	late autumn	early winter	mid winter	late winter	early spring	mid spring	late spring	early summer	mid summer	late summer	early autumn	mid autumn	late autumn	early winter

ABOUT RUNNER BEANS

- Some growers favour sowing the seeds directly into the prepared ground between late spring and early summer. Others opt for an early start by raising seedlings under glass between mid- and late spring, and some do both.
- They can be grown as perennials if you lift and store the roots and the end of one season, and plant them afresh at the beginning of another.
- Supports – wigwams, wire fences, frames and so on – must be very strong and stable.

GROWING MEDIUM

If you want a heavy crop, layer the beds up with lots of well-rotted farmyard manure, garden compost and spent mushroom compost. If your site is windy, set the seeds or plants about 20 cm (8 in) apart and build a super-strong wigwam for maximum support.

SOWING AND PLANTING

- **Early in the year** Excavate the bed, fill it with rotted manure and top it off with a mulch of mushroom compost a few weeks before planting.
- **Mid-spring** Raise seedlings under glass and plant seeds about 2.5 cm (1 in) deep in compost-filled pots (then plant out in late spring to early summer); alternatively, sow seeds directly in the ground. Either way, set them about 15–20 cm (6–8 in) apart over the whole bed.

GENERAL CARE

Pull up large weeds, gently stir the growing medium with a hoe to create a loose mulch and cover with mushroom compost. In very dry weather, spread a mulch of straw or old manure over the whole bed to help hold in the moisture. Pinch out the tips when they reach the top of the frame.

HARVESTING

You can harvest from mid-summer to mid-autumn. Pick every few days rather than once a week. If you allow pods to grow to maturity, the plants will come to a halt.

Growing medium: Very rich and fertile
Situation: Open and sunny
Harvest: Pick regularly before they toughen

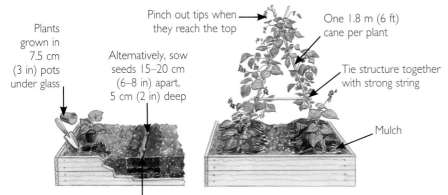

Plants grown in 7.5 cm (3 in) pots under glass

Pinch out tips when they reach the top

Alternatively, sow seeds 15–20 cm (6–8 in) apart, 5 cm (2 in) deep

One 1.8 m (6 ft) cane per plant

Tie structure together with strong string

Mulch

60 cm (2 ft) wide, 23 cm (9 in) deep trench

Troubleshooting

Insect pests Pinch out and remove affected areas and spray with a solution of water and liquid soap.

Blotchy leaves Pull up and burn diseased plants, and avoid planting on the same plot for a couple of years.

Nibbles and notches These are evidence of bean weevil. Avoid the problem by hoeing around the young plants when they are at the two- or three-leaf stage.

Mice Damage shows as nibbles and mess. Set traps.

Withered plants This problem can usually be prevented simply by lots of watering at the flowering stage.

Broad beans

Broad beans are a perfect choice for no-dig raised-bed vegetable gardening – they are hardy, they flourish in tight groups or blocks, they have a long growing season, they crop well, and, best of all, they can easily be stored by freezing or drying.

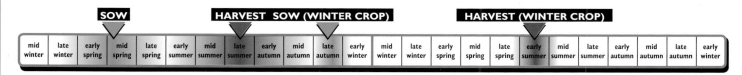

			SOW					HARVEST	SOW (WINTER CROP)								HARVEST (WINTER CROP)						
mid winter	late winter	early spring	mid spring	late spring	early summer	mid summer	late summer	early autumn	mid autumn	late autumn	early winter	mid winter	late winter	early spring	mid spring	late spring	early summer	mid summer	late summer	early autumn	mid autumn	late autumn	early winter

Early: Rich and moisture-retentive with well-rotted manure added
Main: Less manure, add sand
Situation: Airy
Harvest: Pick when beans are formed inside pods

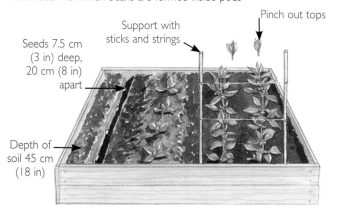

Seeds 7.5 cm (3 in) deep, 20 cm (8 in) apart

Support with sticks and strings

Pinch out tops

Depth of soil 45 cm (18 in)

BROAD BEAN FACTS

- Broad beans are known variously around the world as fava beans, field beans, bell beans and tic beans.
- If you sow in mid- to late autumn in year 1, for cropping in the early summer of year 2, and also sow from late winter through to late spring in year 2, then you will be able to eat broad beans the whole summer long, and you will have a good surplus for freezing or drying.
- Overwintered plants seem to be more resistant to blackfly.

GROWING MEDIUM

Broad beans do best in a deep, rich, moisture-retentive soil that has bean enriched with well-rotted farmyard manure. A good starting point is to increase the depth of the raised bed to about 45 cm (18 in), and then increase the amount of manure for the early crop, and reduce the manure and add a bit of sand for the main crop. Generally, you should choose beds that are in a light, airy spot.

SOWING AND PLANTING

- **Late winter through to mid-spring** Sow main crop in sandy soil. Prepare 7.5 cm (3 in) deep drills or dibbed holes and sow single seeds about 20 cm (8 in) apart in all directions. Water.
- **Winter-hardy crop through late autumn** Sow as above.
- Pick a sunny spot – and a bed which did not have beans growing in it in the previous year.

GENERAL CARE

When the plants are a few centimetres high, draw the soil around the stems and add a thin mulch of well-rotted manure over the whole bed. As soon as the flowers are well formed, pinch out the top shoots; this will plump up the pods and hold back the blackfly. Ring the bed with sticks and string so that the whole block of plants is well supported.

HARVESTING

Depending on the variety and the planting date, you can harvest between early summer and mid-autumn. When the beans are firm, tweak the pods from the stem. When the crop is finished, cut the plant right down to the ground to leave the roots in the soil.

Troubleshooting

Wind damage Make sure that each bed or block of plants is well supported with sticks and string, plus, if the wind is bad, ring the bed with close-mesh screen of plastic mesh or even with woven willow panels.

Blackfly Pinch out and remove badly affected areas, and spray the plant with a solution of water and soap liquid.

Nibbles and notches Nibbles around the leaf edges are caused by the bean weevil. Avoid the problem by spraying with an organic mix and by hoeing the area around the young plants.

Sweetcorn

Also known as Indian corn, sugar corn, pole corn, maize and many other names, sweetcorn was not so long ago thought by many gardeners to be an outlandish item. Now it is commonplace to see fields bulging with the corn on the cob, and most keen gardeners grow it as a maincrop.

				SOW				**HARVEST**															
mid winter	late winter	early spring	mid spring	late spring	early summer	mid summer	late summer	early autumn	mid autumn	late autumn	early winter	mid winter	late winter	early spring	mid spring	late spring	early summer	mid summer	late summer	early autumn	mid autumn	late autumn	early winter

ABOUT SWEETCORN

- Sweetcorn is a good starter crop for interested children.
- Sweetcorn needs a growing season of 70–120 frost-free days after planting.
- Some varieties grow to 1.5–1.8 m (5–6 ft) in height.

GROWING MEDIUM

Sweetcorn likes a well-prepared, deeply worked, well-drained, light to sandy growing medium in a sheltered, sunny position. Dig in plenty of manure and compost in autumn, or grow it in a bed that has been well manured for a previous crop. Sweetcorn needs lots of moisture. If the medium dries out, soak it with water and cover with a mulch of well-rotted spent manure.

SOWING AND PLANTING

- **Mid-spring** Sow 1 seed 2.5 cm (1 in) deep per peat pot, put under glass or plastic and water generously. Alternatively, plant directly in the bed at a grid spacing of 30 cm (1 ft), and protect with clear plastic.
- **Late spring to early summer** Harden the plants off by standing them outside in a sheltered position in the sun for a few days, bringing them inside when the sun goes down. Dig holes 30 cm (1 ft) apart in a grid pattern, and use a fine spray to water the peat pots into place.

GENERAL CARE

Use a hoe to stir the surface of the bed to create a loose mulch, and your fingers to heap the mulch up to support the stems. Be very careful not to damage the stems when the plants are at the young and fragile stage. If the weather turns very dry, water generously and cover the ground with a thick mulch of spent mushroom compost. Protect with a net and give extra water when the cobs start to show. Support any top-heavy plants with poles.

HARVESTING

Harvest from mid-summer to mid-autumn, when the cobs show black-brown, tail-like silks. Test the grains with your nail: if they ooze a milky fluid under pressure, they are ready. Pick the cobs by hand, with a swift twist-and-down action. For maximum taste, texture and sweetness, cook and eat within 10 minutes of harvesting.

Troubleshooting

Distorted growth Probably caused by the frit fly. You will notice distorted leaves, general weak growth and small white maggots inside the young shoots. Avoid the problem next time by growing a different variety on a different bed, and by growing under cover until the plants are beyond the five-leaf stage.

Mushroom-like growths These growths on the cob are probably caused by smut infection. Pull up and burn at the first sign of a problem, use another bed next time, and grow a resistant variety.

Birds and mice Protect the cobs when they begin to swell.

Growing medium: Fertile and well-drained
Situation: Sunny and sheltered
Harvest: When cobs have brown tails/silks

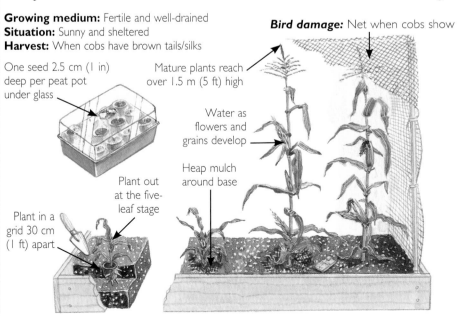

One seed 2.5 cm (1 in) deep per peat pot under glass

Plant in a grid 30 cm (1 ft) apart

Plant out at the five-leaf stage

Mature plants reach over 1.5 m (5 ft) high

Water as flowers and grains develop

Heap mulch around base

Bird damage: Net when cobs show

Onions and shallots

If, like many people, you eat onions on a daily basis – in stir-fries, soups, salads, pickles, chutney, sandwiches, stews and so on – why not increase your options and potential by growing a whole range of varieties of onions and shallots? They can easily be stored for use whenever you want them.

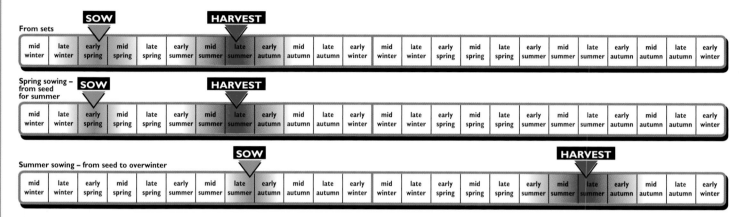

From sets — SOW (early spring) · HARVEST (late summer)

mid winter	late winter	early spring	mid spring	late spring	early summer	mid summer	late summer	early autumn	mid autumn	late autumn	early winter	mid winter	late winter	early spring	mid spring	late spring	early summer	mid summer	late summer	early autumn	mid autumn	late autumn	early winter

Spring sowing – from seed for summer — SOW (late winter) · HARVEST (late summer)

mid winter	late winter	early spring	mid spring	late spring	early summer	mid summer	late summer	early autumn	mid autumn	late autumn	early winter	mid winter	late winter	early spring	mid spring	late spring	early summer	mid summer	late summer	early autumn	mid autumn	late autumn	early winter

Summer sowing – from seed to overwinter — SOW (late summer) · HARVEST (late summer)

mid winter	late winter	early spring	mid spring	late spring	early summer	mid summer	late summer	early autumn	mid autumn	late autumn	early winter	mid winter	late winter	early spring	mid spring	late spring	early summer	mid summer	late summer	early autumn	mid autumn	late autumn	early winter

ABOUT ONIONS AND SHALLOTS

- Onions can be grown from seed or sets. Sets are expensive, and seeds take lots of time but cost less.

Growing medium: Light, well-drained
Situation: Sunny
Harvest: When they die back naturally

- Shallots are planted singly – when they are planted in spring, they grow to produce a hand-sized cluster.

GROWING MEDIUM

Onions do best on a deeply worked, well-manured, moist, well-drained, friable, fertile, sandy growing medium in a sunny position.

SOWING AND PLANTING PROCEDURES

- Sow / plant according to the calendar.
- Sow 6 mm (¼ in) deep in boxes under cover, thin out when big enough to handle, and plant out in the beds on a 7.5–10 cm (3–4 in) grid when the plants are the size of slender pencils.
- Dig holes about 2.5 cm (1 in) deep, trim roots down to 2.5 cm (1 in), trim the leaves to remove the yellow tips, and water the onions into the holes.

GENERAL CARE

Hoe the surface to create a loose mulch. When the swelling bulb begins to show, draw the medium slightly away so the bulb sits high on the surface. Do not water, but keep hoeing the ground.

HARVESTING

Harvest from early summer to early autumn. Lift salad onions and large onions as needed. To ripen, when the plants begin to die back bend the tops over. When they start to turn yellow, ease the onions from the ground and leave them to dry on nets or racks.

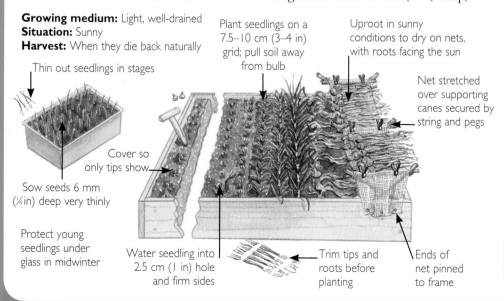

Thin out seedlings in stages

Cover so only tips show

Sow seeds 6 mm (¼ in) deep very thinly

Protect young seedlings under glass in midwinter

Plant seedlings on a 7.5–10 cm (3–4 in) grid; pull soil away from bulb

Water seedling into 2.5 cm (1 in) hole and firm sides

Trim tips and roots before planting

Uproot in sunny conditions to dry on nets, with roots facing the sun

Net stretched over supporting canes secured by string and pegs

Ends of net pinned to frame

Troubleshooting

Yellow, drooping leaves Probably caused by onion fly. If at any time you see maggots in the stem and/or bulb, pull up and burn the plant.

Dark green, drooping leaves These suggest that there is too much nitrogen in the growing medium. Avoid the problem next time by only using well-rotted manure.

Orange-brown blotches Probably caused by rust. Spray with an organic mix, and if this does not work pull up and burn affected plants. Try planting disease-resistant varieties next time.

Leeks

If you want a really tasty item, leeks are wonderful – you can enjoy them tender and raw, cooked in soups, or chopped, steamed and served with olive oil and fresh bread, for example. The plants seem to be able to withstand any extreme of weather from wind and rain to snow and severe frosts.

SOW		PLANT									HARVEST												
mid winter	late winter	early spring	mid spring	late spring	early summer	mid summer	late summer	early autumn	mid autumn	late autumn	early winter	mid winter	late winter	early spring	mid spring	late spring	early summer	mid summer	late summer	early autumn	mid autumn	late autumn	early winter

ABOUT LEEKS

- Leeks are grown and tended in much the same way as celery – they need a long growing season.
- Traditionally, gardeners thought that leeks improved heavy soil.
- Because they can stand frosts, leeks are a very good option for winter use, when other vegetables are scarce.
- Varieties range from small and mild to large and strong-tasting. Carefully choose a variety to suit both your tastes and your location.
- If you get it right, every plant will give you 0.5 kg (1 lb) or so of edible leek – or, put another way, it will feed two hungry adults.

GROWING MEDIUM

Leeks can be grown in an open site on just about any soil, but if you are after a really good fertile crop your growing medium needs to be of a good depth, well manured and moist (meaning that, while the growing medium within the bed feels damp to the touch, the ground around and under the bed is well drained). The drainage specifics need emphasizing, because, if you get it wrong, the hearts will rot out.

SOWING AND PLANTING

- **Mid- to late winter or early to mid-spring (depending on variety)** Sow about 6 mm (¼ in) deep in trays and keep under glass or plastic. Prick out to 5 cm (2 in) apart.
- **Mid-summer** On a showery day, dib 15 cm (6 in) deep holes at 15–20 cm (6–8 in) intervals on a grid to give you 25–30 plants to a 90 cm (3 ft) square bed. Drop one seedling into each dibbed hole and gently top up with water.

GENERAL CARE

Stir the surface of the growing medium with a hoe to create a loose mulch. Along the way the dibbed holes will gradually fill with loose medium to support and blanch the growing plants. Once the transplanted seedlings are well established, surround them with a mulch of chopped straw or old spent manure, and spend time every week with the hoe drawing the earth up. Repeat this procedure throughout the season until all but the tops of the plants are covered. Alternatievly, add extra frames on the bed and top up with mulches, so that the stems are always covered. Water frequently.

HARVESTING

You can harvest from early autumn to late spring – the precise time depends on your chosen variety and growing methods. Use a fork to help ease the roots from the ground, and lift as needed.

Growing medium: Rich, moist and free-draining
Situation: Open
Harvest when needed: Lever with a fork to loosen soil

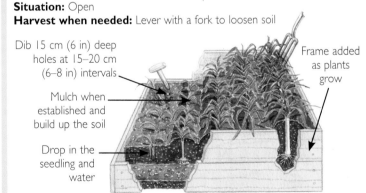

Dib 15 cm (6 in) deep holes at 15–20 cm (6–8 in) intervals

Frame added as plants grow

Mulch when established and build up the soil

Drop in the seedling and water

Troubleshooting

Yellow drooping leaves Most likely caused by onion fly, and shows as yellow leaves and maggots in the stem and roots. Pull up and burn badly affected plants.

Sagging stems This suggests that the plants need additional earthing up.

Orange-brown blotches Probably caused by rust. Pull up and burn affected plants at the first sign of a problem.

Dark green, drooping leaves Too much nitrogen. Avoid the problem by only using well-rotted manure.

Garlic

Many people love eating garlic in soups, stews, stir-fries, salads and numerous other dishes. One of best ways to enjoy it is to sprinkle finely chopped garlic on toast that has been drenched in high-quality olive oil. It is also very good for you – eating raw garlic is reputed to ward off colds.

PLANT   **HARVEST**

mid winter	late winter	early spring	mid spring	late spring	early summer	mid summer	late summer	early autumn	mid autumn	late autumn	early winter	mid winter	late winter	early spring	mid spring	late spring	early summer	mid summer	late summer	early autumn	mid autumn	late autumn	early winter

ABOUT GARLIC

- Garlic is grown in much the same way as onion sets – the cloves are set just below the surface, and they like a rich, moist, well-drained growing medium in a warm, sunny position.
- Despite all the mysterious folk tales surrounding garlic, it is surprisingly simple to grow.
- Garlic is very easy to store. You just string it up, like onions, and store it in a cool, dry room or shed.
- You can plant and grow garlic cloves saved from your own crop, but cloves from shop-bought garlic do not seem to flourish.

GROWING MEDIUM

Garlic likes a light growing medium that contains plenty of well-rotted manure from a previous crop. Make sure when you are planning where to grow your garlic that you select a well-drained bed that is positioned in a warm, sunny corner – perhaps against the wall of the house or in the sunny lea of a shed.

SOWING AND PLANTING

- **Autumn or early spring** Plant single cloves 10–15 cm (4–6 in) deep, in a grid pattern that sets the mature plants about 15–20 cm (6–8 in) apart. Compact the growing medium over the clove and water generously.
- When the shoots begin to appear, use your fingertips to ease the medium gently up and around the plant to protect it.

Growing medium: Rich, moist and well drained
Situation: Sunny
Harvest: When leaves turn yellow

Spring clamps or pegs

Cover developing plants to prevent birds pecking them up

Sticks laid across support the net

Plant single cloves 10–15 cm (4–6 in) deep and 15–20 cm (6–8 in) apart

Fork up the bulb and leave in sun to dry

- Water generously throughout the growing period, but never allow the plants to sit in a puddle of water.

GENERAL CARE

Every day or so, gently stir the surface of the growing medium with a hoe to create a loose mulch, maybe add a thin mulch of spent manure to keep the weeds down, and lightly water. Birds are attracted by the shoots to the extent that they will sometimes pull the little cloves out of the ground. You can prevent this by covering the bed with a net.

HARVESTING

When ready to harvest, sometime in late summer when the green foliage has fallen over and died back, use a small fork to ease the bulbs from the ground. Dry them in the sun, and string them up and store in a cool, dry place, just like onions.

Troubleshooting

Bolting This is caused by alternating wet-drought conditions and/or too much shade. Avoid the problem next time by watering little and often, and choosing beds that are in full sun.

Birds These can be a real nuisance when the green buds are just appearing. Avoid the problem by netting the crop until the plants are well established.

White rot A squashy white rot appears on the bulbs. Burn the affected bulbs and plant in a fresh bed next time.

Potatoes

Most people love potatoes. It may not make economical sense to grow your own, when you can buy them cheaply from a supermarket, but when you have a plate of tasty new potatoes, freshly cooked with mint and a dab of butter or dribble of olive oil, you will be very glad that you did.

	PLANT		▼			HARVEST	▼																	
mid winter	late winter	early spring	mid spring	late spring	early summer	mid summer	late summer	early autumn	mid autumn	late autumn	early winter	mid winter	late winter	early spring	mid spring	late spring	early summer	mid summer	late summer	early autumn	mid autumn	late autumn	early winter

ABOUT POTATOES

- Potatoes are rich in vitamin C.
- The fibre content of a potato complete with skin equals that of many wholegrain cereals.

GROWING MEDIUM

Although just about any growing medium will support potatoes, the make-up of the medium in the garden contributes to the final flavour and texture of the potato on the plate. For example, a heavy, wet mix tends to result in a slick, soapy, slightly yellow potato, while potatoes grown on a dry, sandy medium are often loose and fluffy. As for the underlying soil conditions, a badly drained bed will produce good potatoes in a hot, dry year, but the potatoes will suffer if the weather becomes humid. Potatoes do best in a well-drained, clay to sandy bed, with plenty of mulches of well-rotted manure from a previous crop, in an open, sunny position.

SOWING AND PLANTING

- **Chitting for early crop** In late winter, sit the seed potatoes, rose end up, in

trays in a light, airy shed, until they produce a few 2.5 cm (1 in) shoots.
- **Sowing early** In early to mid-spring, dig 15 cm (6 in) deep holes, 30–40 cm (12–16 in) apart – say four potatoes in a 90 cm (3 ft) square bed – and set the seed potatoes in place so that the shoots are uppermost. Cover them.
- **Sowing under plastic** In early to mid-spring, set the chitted seed potatoes on the surface of the bed 30–40 cm (12–16 in) apart as above, mulch with well-rotted garden compost and cover with black plastic sheet buried at the edges. When the shoots begin to push up against the plastic, cut slits at each planting point to allow the shoots to emerge.

GENERAL CARE

As soon as the foliage appears, mulch with well-rotted mushroom compost. Repeat this so that the foliage is always just about visible. If the weather turns frosty, cover with newspaper or fleece. In very hot weather, stir the surface of the bed with a hoe. Always be on the lookout for slugs. If the weather is very dry, spread a mulch of spent manure

or chopped straw around the plants to hold in the residual moisture.

HARVESTING

Harvest from early summer to mid-autumn. Lift earlies when the flowers are fully open; otherwise wait until the tops have died down. To harvest, take a fork, push it down towards what you estimate is the outer limits of the clump, and gently undermine and lift the whole plant. Leave the potatoes on the surface until the end of the session, and then sort them into 'good' and 'damaged'. Eat the damaged ones first. Lift new potatoes as needed. Store maincrop potatoes in shallow boxes in a dry, dark, frost-free shed.

Troubleshooting

Brown blotchy leaves Probably caused by potato blight. Lift and burn the crop. Avoid the problem next time by using resistant seed and planting in a different bed.

Squashy potatoes This is most likely caused by lack of water and/or repeated wet-dry-wet-dry conditions.

Growing medium: Deep, fertile and well-drained
Situation: Open and sunny
Harvest: Earlies when flowers are fully open; others when tops have died down

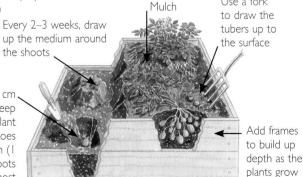

Chitting: tubers should be rose end up

Every 2–3 weeks, draw up the medium around the shoots

Mulch

Use a fork to draw the tubers up to the surface

Dig 15 cm (6 in) deep holes; plant seed potatoes with 2.5 cm (1 in) long shoots uppermost

Add frames to build up depth as the plants grow

Protect from frost with fleece if frost is forecast

Carrots

Carrots are a treat to the eye, they smell and taste good, they can be eaten cooked or raw, they are relatively easy to grow, they can be stored for long periods, they are wonderfully easy to prepare, most children like them, and they can be eaten from early summer to early winter.

SOW **HARVEST**

mid winter	late winter	early spring	mid spring	late spring	early summer	mid summer	late summer	early autumn	mid autumn	late autumn	early winter	mid winter	late winter	early spring	mid spring	late spring	early summer	mid summer	late summer	early autumn	mid autumn	late autumn	early winter

ABOUT CARROTS

- Small 'baby' carrots are certainly juicy and succulent, but mature carrots are generally preferred when the need is for a strong taste and a good bite and texture.
- If you take care when choosing varieties, and if you are willing to protect the plants from weather extremes, you can be eating carrots for the greater part of the year.
- Deep-rooted varieties need a double-depth bed.

GROWING MEDIUM

Carrots thrive on a rich, friable, well-drained, slightly sandy medium in a sunny position. If you want to grow long-rooted types, make sure that the medium is well manured at a greater depth and the overall texture is crumbly; otherwise go for a heavy mix that has been well manured for a previous crop. If your growing medium is stony and/or stiff with fresh manure, the growing roots will divide, giving you stunted and forked carrots that are difficult to prepare.

SOWING AND PLANTING

- **Early spring to early summer (depending on variety)**
  Sow seeds in 18 mm (¾ in) deep drills, 13–15 cm (5–6 in) apart across the width of the bed. Sow thinly, compact the growing medium, and water with a fine sprinkler.
- When the seedlings are big enough to handle, thin them out so they are about 5 cm (2 in) apart. Do this in the evening and remove the debris from the plot.
- Use cloches – glass, corrugated plastic or plastic polytunnel – to protect the plants at both ends of the season.

GENERAL CARE

Ring the bed with a protective barrier of fine netting or clear plastic sheet. Hoe every day or so to get rid of the weeds and to loosen up the surface of the bed. The resulting loose mulch helps to hold in the moisture, which in turn prevents the roots from splitting. In extra-dry weather, increase the watering and spread an additional mulch of spent mushroom compost or garden compost over the whole bed.

HARVESTING

If you make successive sowings of a range of varieties, and protect them with a mulch of chopped straw or spent mushroom compost, you can harvest from late spring to early winter. Pull the carrots up by hand. Pack maincrop carrots in boxes of sand, and store them in a frost-free shed.

Growing medium: Well-drained, friable and slightly sandy
Situation: Sunny
Harvest: Pull by hand while easing with a fork

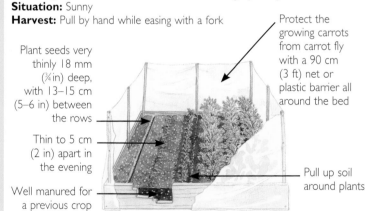

Plant seeds very thinly 18 mm (¾ in) deep, with 13–15 cm (5–6 in) between the rows

Thin to 5 cm (2 in) apart in the evening

Well manured for a previous crop

Protect the growing carrots from carrot fly with a 90 cm (3 ft) net or plastic barrier all around the bed

Pull up soil around plants

Troubleshooting

Soggy holes Probably caused by carrot fly. Limit the problem by growing onions alongside the carrots and by using a 90 cm (3 ft) high barrier of netting or plastic.

Splitting Generally caused by alternating wet-dry-wet conditions. Avoid the problem by spreading a mulch of spent manure to retain residual moisture.

Green top Usually caused by the top or 'shoulders' of the carrot standing proud of the growing medium. Prevent it by hoeing the medium high up around the growing carrots.

Parsnips

In times past, the good old parsnip was served up in place of the potato. They are not as versatile, maybe, but parsnips can be grown in just about any well-prepared fertile soil, they can be left in the ground over winter, and they taste amazingly good when roasted in oil or butter.

SOW   **HARVEST**

mid winter	late winter	early spring	mid spring	late spring	early summer	mid summer	late summer	early autumn	mid autumn	late autumn	early winter	mid winter	late winter	early spring	mid spring	late spring	early summer	mid summer	late summer	early autumn	mid autumn	late autumn	early winter

ABOUT PARSNIPS

- Parsnips are hardy in all but the deepest frost, and generally easy to grow.
- The seeds take quite a long time to germinate and, once through, the seedlings are minute – so be patient, and do not be hasty to replant what you might see as a dud crop.
- You could maximize your space by intercropping with a swift-growing crop such as lettuces or radishes.
- Parsnips are less prone to pests and diseases than potatoes.
- They can be left in the ground over winter and lifted and eaten from mid-autumn around to the following spring. If the weather turns extra cold, cover the bed with a thick 'mattress' mulch of chopped straw.

GROWING MEDIUM

Parsnips do well on just about any well-prepared, friable, fine-textured, well-drained, fertile growing medium. Choose a deep bed so that the roots can go straight down without obstruction. You can either layer up a purpose-made bed with mulches of well-rotted horse manure, or use a bed that has been well manured for a preceding crop. Be warned, however, that if you try to grow them in fresh manure the growing roots will, just like carrots, hit fresh manure and then either fork or become cankered.

SOWING AND PLANTING

- **Late winter to mid-spring** Sow a pinch of seeds in 12 mm (½ in) deep dibbed holes on a 13–15 cm (5–6 in) grid across the bed. Compact the growing medium and water generously with a fine spray. Be careful not to puddle the area.
- When the seedlings are big enough to handle, pinch out to leave a single strong plant at each station.

GENERAL CARE

Stir the surface of the growing medium to create a loose mulch, or remove weeds by hand and cover the ground with a mulch of spent mushroom compost. Either way, you must be extra careful that you do not scrape the 'shoulders' of the root, as such damage might start top-rot or canker. Water little and often (never so much that the bed puddles or leaks water). If the weather turns icy, spread a mulch of chopped straw to give some protection against frost.

Growing medium: Friable, well-drained and fertile
Situation: Open and sunny
Harvest: Lever with a fork to loosen the surrounding soil

Troubleshooting

Parsnip canker This shows itself as a rusty brown mess around the 'shoulders' and is usually caused by physical damage to the root and/or contact with fresh manure. Only use well-rotted manure, and be careful not to touch the roots with the hoe.

Fresh manure Some suppliers do not seem to understand just what 'well-rotted' means and their manure is too fresh. If in doubt, simply take delivery and stack it up for next season.

Fanging This shows as a forked root, generally caused by the presence of fresh manure and/or lots of stones. Remove all stones and avoid using fresh manure.

Splitting This is generally caused by irregular watering.

HARVESTING

You can harvest from mid-autumn to early spring. In all but the coldest and wet winters, parsnips can be left in the ground until they are needed. Ease them up with a fork, being careful not to break off the long root tips.

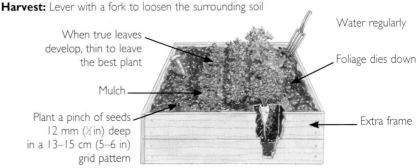

When true leaves develop, thin to leave the best plant

Water regularly

Foliage dies down

Mulch

Plant a pinch of seeds 12 mm (½ in) deep in a 13–15 cm (5–6 in) grid pattern

Extra frame

Beetroot

Colourful, sweet in flavour, slightly crunchy but juicy in texture, and enjoyably easy to grow, beetroot is not only the perfect companion to salads but also very tasty as a hot vegetable. Beetroot can easily be stored by bottling it in a mixture of sugar and vinegar.

				SOW				HARVEST																		
mid winter	late winter	early spring	mid spring	late spring	early summer	mid summer	late summer	early autumn	mid autumn	late autumn	early winter	mid winter	late winter	early spring	mid spring	late spring	early summer	mid summer	late summer	early autumn	mid autumn	late autumn	early winter			

ABOUT BEETROOT

- Newly planted beetroot does not like to be disturbed or checked, so be extra careful when weeding, thinning and spreading a mulch.
- With beetroot, swift and young equates with texture and taste. Ideally, you need to pick the beetroots when they are young and tender, and cook and eat them within an hour or so of picking.
- You must carefully scrub and wash the roots prior to cooking; otherwise the food on your plate will taste dull and muddy.
- As my granny used to say, lazy bowels love beetroot!

GROWING MEDIUM

Beetroot is best grown in a light mix of well-rotted spent manure, old compost and sand. The ground needs to be well drained and well manured, but the manure must not be fresh or rank. A good method is to plant the beetroot on a fertile bed that has been manured for a preceding crop.

SOWING AND PLANTING

- **Early spring to early summer** Sow a pinch of 3–4 ready-soaked seeds about 2.5 cm (1 in) deep at 10–13 cm (4–5 in) intervals, so that a 90 cm (3 ft) square bed contains 36–40 plants. Compact the bed and water generously.
- When the seedlings are big enough to handle, carefully pinch out to leave the strongest plant.
- Firm the ground around the stems of the remaining plants, and water generously with a fine spray.

GENERAL CARE

Spread a web of black cotton threads over and around the bed, or circle it with a net, to keep off birds. Gently stir the surface of the bed with a hoe to create a loose mulch and to keep it free from weeds. If the weather is dry, spread a mulch of spent manure to further hold in the moisture, and water frequently.

HARVESTING

You can harvest from late spring through to late autumn – the time depends on the variety and growing methods. You can start harvesting by pulling every other young root, so that you can eat them small and tender in salads, and leave the rest to grow to a large size. Gently ease the roots from the ground. Twist the leaves off about 5 cm (2 in) above the crown, and eat fresh cooked, or store in boxes of sand.

Growing medium:
Well-drained, well-rotted manure
Situation: Open and sunny

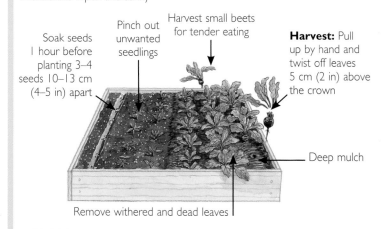

Soak seeds 1 hour before planting 3–4 seeds 10–13 cm (4–5 in) apart

Pinch out unwanted seedlings

Harvest small beets for tender eating

Harvest: Pull up by hand and twist off leaves 5 cm (2 in) above the crown

Deep mulch

Remove withered and dead leaves

Troubleshooting

Splitting roots This is usually caused by long spells of dry weather, and the problem can be avoided by covering the ground with a deep mulch of old spent manure.

Bolting This is usually caused by lack of water. You can avoid the difficulty by spreading a mulch of spent manure or chopped straw, and by generous watering.

Slugs Use slug barriers or traps and/or remove the slugs by hand.

Swedes

Swedes are easy to grow. If you have had trouble growing potatoes, and are looking to grow another primary bulk-food type of crop, they are a good option. A plate of mashed swedes with bread and butter on the side, topped with fried eggs, was favoured by pilots in the Second World War.

SOW (above late spring)   **HARVEST** (above early winter)

mid winter	late winter	early spring	mid spring	late spring	early summer	mid summer	late summer	early autumn	mid autumn	late autumn	early winter	mid winter	late winter	early spring	mid spring	late spring	early summer	mid summer	late summer	early autumn	mid autumn	late autumn	early winter

ABOUT SWEDES

- As swedes belong to the cabbage family, they are affected by many of the same diseases and pests.
- Do not be tempted to grow giant varieties (unless you keep goats); it is much better to choose the smaller types.
- Although swedes are thought to be so hardy that they can be left in the ground over winter, they do better in long periods of frost if they are protected with a thick mulch of chopped straw.
- If you are a vegetarian, try swedes steamed, bashed and buttered. If you eat meat, try them boiled with a ham hock.

GROWING MEDIUM

Swedes do best on a slightly sandy but rich growing medium, meaning a bed that is moisture-retentive and rich with mulches of well-rotted manure that have been sprinkled with sand. Above all, the bed must be moist, because if it dries the plants will swiftly bolt without swelling at the root. However, the bed must not be mushy and/or puddled with standing water. Swedes do best in an open, semi-shaded position with shelter to the windward side.

SOWING AND PLANTING

- **Mid-spring to early summer** Sow seeds in 12 mm (½ in) deep dibbed holes, about 23 cm (9 in) apart. Sow a pinch of seeds in each hole, cover and compact the growing medium and use a fine spray to water generously.
- When the seedlings are big enough to handle, pinch out to leave the strongest plant at each station.
- Water after thinning and use your fingertips to firm the growing medium up around the remaining plants.

GENERAL CARE

Stir the surface of the growing medium with a hoe to create a loose mulch. Be very careful that you do not graze the emerging root, as such damage might well result in top-rot or canker. Water little and often to avoid the flood-drought-flood conditions that cause root splitting.

HARVESTING

You can harvest from early autumn to early spring. Lift the roots as needed. In very cold weather, cover the whole bed with a mulch of chopped straw topped with a sheet of plastic – some sort of waterproof covering that you can swiftly remove to give the plants an airing.

Growing medium: Light and moisture-retentive
Situation: Open and semi-shaded
Harvest: Pull from soil as needed

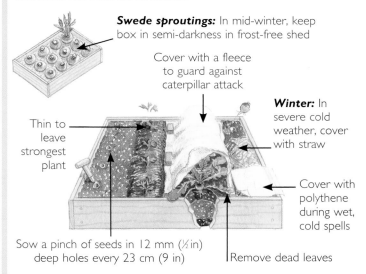

Swede sproutings: In mid-winter, keep box in semi-darkness in frost-free shed

Cover with a fleece to guard against caterpillar attack

Winter: In severe cold weather, cover with straw

Thin to leave strongest plant

Cover with polythene during wet, cold spells

Sow a pinch of seeds in 12 mm (½ in) deep holes every 23 cm (9 in)

Remove dead leaves

Troubleshooting

Slugs and snails Damage shows as holes in leaves and roots. Be aware that slugs and snails can halt tender young plants. Remove the pests by hand on a daily basis.

Big foliage, little roots This indicates that there is too much nitrogen in the growing medium. Avoid the problem by only using well-rotted manure.

Cabbage white butterflies These insects love the leaves, so protect the crop with fleece (as for cabbages).

Turnips

Forget any bad memories of turnips you may have from your school-dinner days – the small, modern, tender varieties of turnip are beautiful. They are soft and white in texture and delicate in taste – wonderful in stews and curries.

SOW Depending on variety **HARVEST**

mid winter	late winter	early spring	mid spring	late spring	early summer	mid summer	late summer	early autumn	mid autumn	late autumn	early winter	mid winter	late winter	early spring	mid spring	late spring	early summer	mid summer	late summer	early autumn	mid autumn	late autumn	early winter

ABOUT TURNIPS

- Small, fast-growing varieties can be sown as catch crops between rows of slow-growing vegetables.
- Turnips grown for their tops are sown in late summer for eating in early spring. They are very tasty!
- Turnips belong to the cabbage family, so are affected by similar pests and diseases.

GROWING MEDIUM

Turnips, just like swedes, do well on a rich, light, sandy, moisture-retentive growing medium that has been well manured with rotted compost. If your plot is extra dry, and/or you fail to water regularly, there is a good chance that the roots will falter and the plants bolt and come to nothing. Avoid a bed that looks to be sticky and/or puddled with standing water. Turnips do best in an open, semi-shaded bed that has plenty of shelter to the windward side.

SOWING AND PLANTING

- Sow seeds in late winter to early summer, or mid-summer to early autumn, depending on variety. Sow a pinch of seed in 12 mm (½ in) deep dibbed holes, 15–20 cm (6–8 in) apart, and cover. Firm in and water generously.
- When the seedlings are big enough to handle, pinch out to leave a single strong plant at each station. Water before and after thinning. Use your fingers to firm the growing medium up around the young plants.

GENERAL CARE

Stir the surface of the growing medium with your fingers to create a loose mulch. Be careful not to damage the turnips' 'shoulders', as this might result in top-rot or canker. Water little and often. If it turns very dry, give the bed a good slow soaking and mulch thickly with spent mushroom compost.

HARVESTING

You can, depending on variety, harvest the roots from mid-autumn to early winter, and the tops from early to mid-spring. Lift the roots as needed. Turnips are best eaten small, young and tender.

Growing medium: Light and moisture-retentive
Situation: Open and semi-shaded
Harvest: Pull from soil as needed when small and tender

Winter varieties: Harvest young leaves in early summer to eat as greens

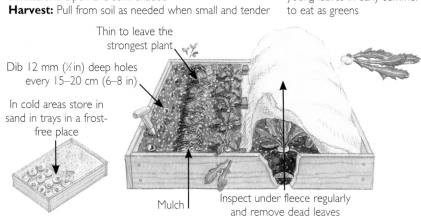

Thin to leave the strongest plant

Dib 12 mm (½ in) deep holes every 15–20 cm (6–8 in)

In cold areas store in sand in trays in a frost-free place

Mulch

Inspect under fleece regularly and remove dead leaves

Troubleshooting

Slugs and snails You will find holes in the leaves and damage to the roots. Too many slugs and snails can halt the growth of the young plants. Remove the pests by hand on a daily basis.

Canker Usually reveals itself as a rusty brown mess around the 'shoulders' of the root. The problem can be caused by physical damage to the root, and/or contact with fresh manure, so only use well-rotted manure, and be careful not to scratch or graze the roots.

Clubroot This shows as distorted roots. Pull up and burn affected plants.

Radishes

Radishes are extremely good as a swift fill-in or intercrop. Sprinkle the seeds around your more slow-growing crops, such as lettuces, parsnips, cabbages and cauliflowers, water daily, wait for a few weeks and you have the perfect crispy-crunchy salad bite to go with your bread and cheese.

			SOW					HARVEST																
mid winter	late winter	early spring	mid spring	late spring	early summer	mid summer	late summer	early autumn	mid autumn	late autumn	early winter	mid winter	late winter	early spring	mid spring	late spring	early summer	mid summer	late summer	early autumn	mid autumn	late autumn	early winter

ABOUT RADISHES

- The generic name for radishes, *Raphanus*, comes from the Greek *raphanos*, meaning 'quickly appearing'.
- Radishes can easily be grown all year round in temperate regions.
- The secret of growing a swift, plump crop is to choose the appropriate variety – for location and season – and sow the seeds thinly in a rich, moist growing medium.
- Never allow radishes to be short of water – they need watering a lot and often. Pick them as soon as they are ready so that they do not become old and woody.
- Children enjoy the fast results.

GROWING MEDIUM

Radishes thrive on a rich, moist, fertile growing medium in a sunny, open position. Ideally, the bed needs to be porous, easily worked and rich in old, well-rotted manure from previous crops. If the bed is overly rich in fresh manure, you will probably get fast-growing leafy plants that are small, tough and stringy at the root – they may be good on the eye but are not much fun to eat. Make sure that you compact the surface of the bed before and after sowing, so that the roots plump up.

SOWING AND PLANTING

- **Mid-winter to late summer** Sow seeds in succession every week or so in 12 mm (½ in) deep drills, 10–15 cm (4–6 in) apart. Compact the growing medium and water generously.
- When the seedlings are big enough to handle, thin to leave the strongest plants about 2.5 cm (1 in) apart. Water generously before and after thinning.

GENERAL CARE

Stir the surface of the growing medium with a hoe at each side of the row to create a loose mulch. Water little and often to avoid the wet-drought-wet conditions that cause root splitting. If the weather turns dry, use your fingers to spread a thin mulch of spent manure around the growing plants.

HARVESTING

You can harvest from mid-spring to late winter, the precise length of time depending on variety and growing methods. Pull them up when they are small, young and tender and eat them as soon as possible after pulling.

Growing medium: Moist and fertile
Situation: Open and sunny
Harvest: By pulling them from the ground by hand

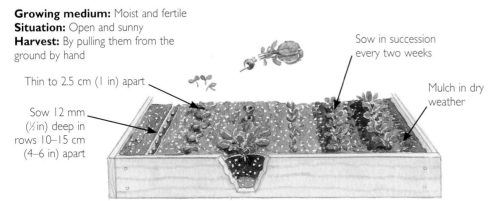

Thin to 2.5 cm (1 in) apart

Sow 12 mm (½ in) deep in rows 10–15 cm (4–6 in) apart

Sow in succession every two weeks

Mulch in dry weather

Troubleshooting

Slugs and snails Damage shows as slimy holes in leaves and roots. Harvest regularly and remove the pests by hand on a daily basis.

Big foliage, little roots Probably caused by too much nitrogen in fresh manure. Avoid the problem by only using well-rotted manure.

Artichokes, Jerusalem

The Jerusalem artichoke, also called sunroot and sunchoke, is very easy to grow. It produces a soaring mass of foliage, large, yellow, daisy-like flowers, and knobby, potato-like tubers. As for taste, if you think 'nutty' potato with a hint of globe artichoke, you will not be far off the mark.

		PLANT							**HARVEST**														
mid winter	late winter	early spring	mid spring	late spring	early summer	mid summer	late summer	early autumn	mid autumn	late autumn	early winter	mid winter	late winter	early spring	mid spring	late spring	early summer	mid summer	late summer	early autumn	mid autumn	late autumn	early winter

ABOUT JERUSALEM ARTICHOKES

- They are grown just like poatoes.
- Some people find them indigestible and wind-making.
- The name Jerusalem is thought to be an American English seventeenth-century derivation of the Italian name *girasole*.
- A healthy plant will grow to a height of 3 m (10 ft) or more, so you must carefully consider where they are going to be planted. (Do you want to use them as a windbreak? Will they cast unwanted shade?)
- If all goes well, each egg-sized tuber will give you a yield of 1–1.5 kg (2–3 1b).
- If you are tempted to grow them as a permanent crop on the same bed, make sure that you lift and select the best tubers, and repeatedly mulch with well-rotted manure.

GROWING MEDIUM

Grown in beds just like potatoes, the Jerusalem artichoke does best in a dry, rich medium that has been well manured for a previous crop. Prepare the bed with layers of well-rotted farmyard manure, with extra mulches in the spring and autumn.

SOWING AND PLANTING

- **Late winter to mid-spring** Plant the tubers about 25 cm (10 in) apart at a depth of about 15 cm (6 in), say 9–11 plants to a 90 cm (3 ft) square bed.

- Tread the plants in well, and water daily until the plant looks to be well established.

GENERAL CARE

As soon as the plants are about 30 cm (1 ft) or so high, use a hoe to earth up, and build some sort of support, using poles, a frame or a fence, up which the plants can grow. The easiest option is a pole-and-wire fence, like for runner beans or raspberries. At some point when the plants are 60–90 cm (2–3 ft) high, spread an extra mulch of spent compost and hoe it so that the tubers are topped by a ridge or mound about 15 cm (6 in) high.

HARVESTING

Harvest from mid-autumn onwards when the flowers and foliage begin to brown and die back. Cut the stems off to within 30 cm (1 ft) or so of the ground, protect with a mulch of chopped straw and lift the tubers as and when needed. Finally, remove all the tubers and keep some for planting next time.

Growing medium: Rich, well-drained
Situation: Warm, well-drained position

Harvest: Dig up as needed

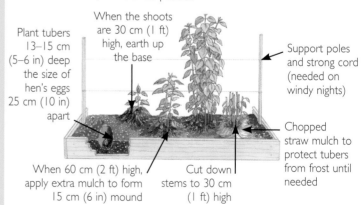

Plant tubers 13–15 cm (5–6 in) deep the size of hen's eggs 25 cm (10 in) apart

When the shoots are 30 cm (1 ft) high, earth up the base

Support poles and strong cord (needed on windy nights)

When 60 cm (2 ft) high, apply extra mulch to form 15 cm (6 in) mound

Cut down stems to 30 cm (1 ft) high

Chopped straw mulch to protect tubers from frost until needed

Troubleshooting

Slugs These can be a real tuber-eating nuisance. Use slug barriers or traps and/or remove the slugs by hand.

Troublesome tubers When lifting, make sure that you completely remove even the smallest tubers, otherwise they will sprout and become weeds.

Celeriac

Although celeriac or turnip-rooted celery is related to celery, the difference is that celery is grown for its crunchy stems and for its heart, whereas celeriac is grown for its turnip-like root. Celeriac is easier to grow than celery, and is delicious in a winter soup or a winter salad.

		SOW			PLANT						HARVEST												
mid winter	late winter	early spring	mid spring	late spring	early summer	mid summer	late summer	early autumn	mid autumn	late autumn	early winter	mid winter	late winter	early spring	mid spring	late spring	early summer	mid summer	late summer	early autumn	mid autumn	late autumn	early winter

ABOUT CELERIAC

- This is a relatively easy-to-grow plant, as long as it is sown under glass, carefully hardened off before planting out in the bed, and kept well watered.
- Celeriac and celery are members of the same botanical family, but they do not come from the same plant.
- Celeriac tastes good when turned into a thin, clear soup, or grated and eaten raw with a salad.

GROWING MEDIUM

Celeriac is much easier to grow than celery in that it is grown on the flat, and it does not need to be earthed up and blanched. It does best in a well-manured medium, with the manure having been put down as a thick mulch in the preceding winter, in a bed in a sunny but sheltered site where it can spend a long, uninterrupted growing season. Make sure when the root is swelling that you keep the plant well watered – give it as much water as possible in dry spells. If you under-water, the swelling roots will perhaps shrink and rot, or at least stop growing.

SOWING AND PLANTING

- **Early to mid-spring** Sow seeds about 12 mm (½ in) deep under glass in prepared seed-trays (they are very slow-growing). As soon as the seedlings are big enough to handle, pot them into peat pots.
- **Late spring to early summer** Plant out 25 cm (10 in) apart, with 12–16 plants in a 90 cm (3 ft) square bed. Set the plants as 'shallow' as possible so that each one is sitting in a saucer-shaped depression.
- Trim the leaves after planting.

Growing medium: Rich, well-manured and moist
Situation: Sunny and sheltered
Harvest: Pull from the ground and remove leaves

GENERAL CARE

Water the plants daily. Stir the surface of the growing medium with a hoe to create a loose mulch and to keep it clean and free from pests. Remove old leaves and any wandering shoots and roots, and generally keep the surface of the bed free from debris. You should never allow the ground to dry out.

HARVESTING

If your site is well drained, and you protect the plants with straw and fleece, you can leave the crop in the ground, and harvest from late autumn to early spring. If your bed is wet, lift the roots and store in a frost-free shed.

> ### *Troubleshooting*
>
> **Rusty-coloured tunnels** Probably caused by carrot fly. Try to avoid the problem by growing onions alongside the celeriac.
>
> **Splitting** Most likely caused by alternating wet-dry conditions. Prevent the problem by spreading a mulch of spent manure to hold in the moisture.
>
> **Slugs** Use slug barriers or traps and/or remove the slugs by hand.

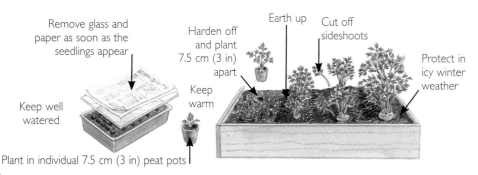

Remove glass and paper as soon as the seedlings appear

Keep well watered

Plant in individual 7.5 cm (3 in) peat pots

Harden off and plant 7.5 cm (3 in) apart

Keep warm

Earth up

Cut off sideshoots

Protect in icy winter weather

Tomatoes (outdoor)

Some beginners to gardening think that tomatoes can only be grown in a greenhouse or polytunnel, but many varieties can be grown outdoors. Tomatoes picked straight from the vine are wonderfully sweet and tasty. The unripened green ones can be used in chutneys and sauces.

		SOW		PLANT		HARVEST																	
mid winter	late winter	early spring	mid spring	late spring	early summer	mid summer	late summer	early autumn	mid autumn	late autumn	early winter	mid winter	late winter	early spring	mid spring	late spring	early summer	mid summer	late summer	early autumn	mid autumn	late autumn	early winter

ABOUT OUTDOOR TOMATOES

- If you get it right, outdoor varieties not only crop more heavily than those grown under glass, but they are also sturdier, healthier and altogether more flavoursome. Outdoor tomatoes tend to have tougher skins, however.
- Bush tomatoes are easier to grow.
- Tomatoes like dry, hot conditions with plenty of watering. The ideal is to site them in full sun, with protection on the shady sides.
- Perhaps more than anything else, tomatoes dislike draughts, uneven watering, and stagnant water.

GROWING MEDIUM

Outdoor tomatoes will do well in just about any bed, as long as the growing medium is of a good depth, richly manured, compact in texture, well drained, and in a sunny but sheltered position.

SOWING AND PLANTING

- **Early to mid-spring** Sow the seeds in a tray of moistened potting compost, and protect with a sheet of glass topped with newspaper. Keep warm.
- **Mid- to late spring** When the seedlings are large enough, prick them out into 7.5 cm (3 in) peat pots. Water and keep warm.
- **Late spring to early summer (after the last frosts)** Set the peat pots 45 cm (18 in) apart in a sheltered bed, water and protect with a cloche or plastic. Plant away from potatoes.

GENERAL CARE

Support the plant with a stake and loose ties. Pinch out the sideshoots. Remove the growing tip when there are 5–6 trusses. When the fruit starts to ripen, mulch with rotted manure topped with a bed of straw. Cover with the cloche and continue to water the roots.

HARVESTING

You can harvest from mid-summer to mid-autumn, the precise time depending on variety. Check that the straw is crisp and dry. Pluck the tomatoes when they are firm and nicely coloured.

Troubleshooting

Discoloured leaves The cause could be lack of water, a virus or even some sort of mildew. If, after a day or so of watering, you see that the foliage is curled and slightly splotchy, it is likely to be mildew or a damaging virus. Strip off the damaged foliage and drench with an organic anti-mildew spray. If all this is has no effect, wait until the remaining fruits ripen, and then pull up and burn the plants. Avoid the problem next time by planting virus-resistant varieties in a different position.

Blight This shows itself as rotten fruit. Pull up and burn affected plants, and use another bed next time. Do not follow the tomatoes with potatoes.

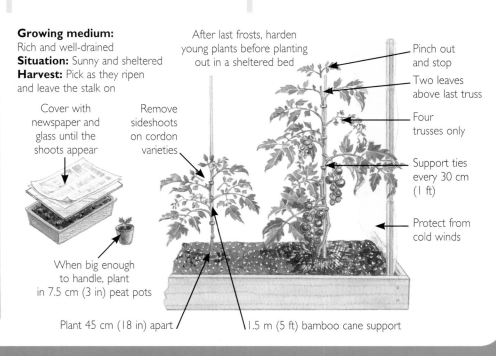

Growing medium: Rich and well-drained
Situation: Sunny and sheltered
Harvest: Pick as they ripen and leave the stalk on

After last frosts, harden young plants before planting out in a sheltered bed

Pinch out and stop

Two leaves above last truss

Four trusses only

Support ties every 30 cm (1 ft)

Protect from cold winds

Cover with newspaper and glass until the shoots appear

Remove sideshoots on cordon varieties

When big enough to handle, plant in 7.5 cm (3 in) peat pots

Plant 45 cm (18 in) apart

1.5 m (5 ft) bamboo cane support

Marrows and courgettes

There are no real disadvantages to growing marrows and courgettes. When they are grown in corners on compost and dung heaps, they make the unsightly both gorgeous and cost-effective. Their shape and speed of growth is surprising, they are incredibly tasty, and they can be frozen.

			SOW	PLANT			HARVEST																
mid winter	late winter	early spring	mid spring	late spring	early summer	mid summer	late summer	early autumn	mid autumn	late autumn	early winter	mid winter	late winter	early spring	mid spring	late spring	early summer	mid summer	late summer	early autumn	mid autumn	late autumn	early winter

ABOUT MARROWS AND COURGETTES

- Courgettes are easier to grow.
- Marrows can be steamed, stuffed, roasted and pickled.
- Courgettes and onions fried in olive oil and served on toast are delicious!
- The golden-yellow variety of courgette looks good on the plate, and has a very firm bite.

GROWING MEDIUM

Marrows and courgettes do best on a deeply worked, well-manured, moist, well-drained growing medium. They always seem to grow well on a compost heap, so either grow them on a heap of well-rotted manure and compost or fill a bed with layered mulches of garden compost, farmyard compost and mushroom compost.

SOWING AND PLANTING

- **Mid- to late spring** Sow two seeds about 18 mm (¾ in) deep in peat pots under glass or plastic. Thin the seedlings to one good plant.

- **Late spring to early summer** When the stems are hairy, dig holes 30 cm (1 ft) deep and 30 cm (1 ft) wide, and set one plant to a 90 cm (3 ft) square bed. Fill a hole with well-rotted manure, cover it with a flat mound of manure topped with a shallow layer of compost, and put the seedling in its peat pot in place. If the growing medium spills over, you might need to add an extra frame to increase the overall depth of the bed.

GENERAL CARE

Stir the surface of the growing medium with a hoe to create a loose mulch. Once the plants are hardened off and under way, cover the mound with a mulch of spent manure to hold in the moisture. When the plants have run or grown out to cover the bed, gently pinch out the end of each leading shoot to cause them to branch. Keep watering and mulching throughout the season – mulch with grass clippings, more spent manure, or anything that will hold in the water and help plump up the crop.

HARVESTING

Harvest from mid-summer to mid-autumn. Cut courgettes every few days. A good option is to harvest, eat what you can and fry the rest with olive oil, onions and tomatoes and put them in the freezer. Cut marrows as needed. At the end of the season, hang them in nets and store in a frost-free shed.

Growing medium: Well-manured and free-draining
Situation: Sunny and sheltered
Courgettes: Harvest with a sharp knife when about 10 cm (4 in) long
Marrows: Harvest 7–8 weeks after planting

Sow two seeds 18 mm (¾ in) deep in peat pots; pinch out to leave the best seedling

Plant out in peat pots when stems become hairy

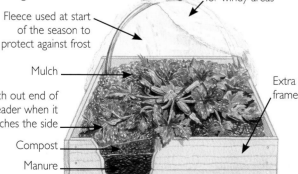

Fleece used at start of the season to protect against frost

Plastic water pipe arches will support a protective cover for windy areas

Mulch

Pinch out end of leader when it reaches the side

Compost

Manure

Extra frame

Rotted manure

Troubleshooting

Slugs and snails Damage appears on young foliage and tender fruits. The best advice is not to plant out the seedlings until they show two good leaves and the stems are hairy. Keep on top of the slugs by tidying up dead leaves and debris, and by removing them by hand on a daily basis.

Mottled leaves Possible sign of mosaic virus. Spray with a soapy water mix to wash off aphids, scrape away and remove the top 2.5 cm (1 in) of growing medium, and remove and burn debris. Avoid the problem by growing a resistant variety on a different bed.

Cucumbers (outdoor or ridge type)

Growing cucumbers outdoors is surprisingly easy, especially if you protect them with some sort of screen. If you want cucumbers with a strong taste and good bite and texture, and are not worried about them being a bit short and lumpy, the outdoor or ridge types are the ones to go for.

Outdoors — SOW | PLANT | HARVEST

mid winter	late winter	early spring	mid spring	late spring	early summer	mid summer	late summer	early autumn	mid autumn	late autumn	early winter	mid winter	late winter	early spring	mid spring	late spring	early summer	mid summer	late summer	early autumn	mid autumn	late autumn	early winter

Indoors — SOW | PLANT | HARVEST

mid winter	late winter	early spring	mid spring	late spring	early summer	mid summer	late summer	early autumn	mid autumn	late autumn	early winter	mid winter	late winter	early spring	mid spring	late spring	early summer	mid summer	late summer	early autumn	mid autumn	late autumn	early winter

ABOUT CUCUMBERS

- In a no-dig garden, the easiest way to grow cucumbers is in a bed protected by a cloche, glass frame or screen.
- Choose a suitable outdoor variety – meaning true ridge or gherkin types.
- If you want to harvest extra early, turn one of your beds into a hotbed by adding huge amounts of fresh stable manure. This is a good option if you can get enough manure.

GROWING MEDIUM

The growing medium needs to be soft, of a good depth, well manured and moist. The easiest way is to build one or more extra-deep beds about 45 cm (18 in) deep and quarter-fill them with fresh stable manure topped with compost and/or well-rotted manure. Choose a sheltered spot in full sun, away from draughts, and build a plastic screen to the windward side. Mound up the growing medium.

SOWING AND PLANTING

- **Mid- to late spring** Sow seeds of outdoor varieties about 18 mm (¾ in) deep directly into 7.5 cm (3 in) peat pots and cover with glass or plastic.
- As soon as the plants have two true leaves, test the bed to make sure that it is not too hot – it needs to be about 18–30°C (64–86°F) – and set them in place, with no more than one plant in a 90 cm (3 ft) square bed.

- Cover the bed with a cloche or screen, or a build a wigwam of sticks and cover it with plastic sheet or fleece.
- Water the plants daily.

GENERAL CARE

If you have made a hotbed, just prior to planting test the temperature to ensure that the bed is not too hot. Nip out the growing point after 5–6 leaves. Water every day and stop the sideshoots when they reach the boundary of their allotted area. Once the small cucumbers begin to show, spread a generous mulch of well-rotted manure over the bed and continue watering copiously.

HARVESTING

Harvest outdoor varieties from early summer to early autumn, depending on variety. Support the weight of the fruit in one hand and cut off with a sharp knife in the other. Gather every other day, and remove yellow leaves, stunted fruits and general debris as you go.

Growing medium: Well-manured and free-draining
Situation: Full sun, sheltered
Harvest: With a sharp knife

Sow 2–3 seeds 18 mm (¾ in) deep in 7.5 cm (3 in) pots

Cover

Plant out when true leaves appear; nip out growing point after 5–6 leaves

Choose the best seedlings and discard the others

Spread out the lateral as they grow; stop them when they reach the sides

Spring clamp or peg

Plastic water pipe and polythene protection

Mulch

Deep bed

Well-rotted manure and compost mound

Quarter-fill with fresh stable manure

Troubleshooting

Withered fruit This could be the result of root rot or some other root problem caused by drought. Remove the damaged fruit and, if you think that lack of water might be a problem, increase the rate of watering

Slugs and snails Shows as damaged trails and pits to the fruit. Remove the pests by hand on a daily basis.

Bitter fruit This is caused by draughty, wet and cold conditions. Water twice daily and surround the plant with a plastic or fleece screen.

Aubergines (Eggplants)

If you can locate a bed in a sunny, sheltered corner, are prepared to spend time building clear plastic screens to make the most of the sun and netted screens to keep off gusty draughts, and you enjoy growing crops such as tomatoes and cucumbers, aubergines are a good choice for you.

SOW → **PLANT** → **HARVEST** →

mid winter	late winter	early spring	mid spring	late spring	early summer	mid summer	late summer	early autumn	mid autumn	late autumn	early winter	mid winter	late winter	early spring	mid spring	late spring	early summer	mid summer	late summer	early autumn	mid autumn	late autumn	early winter

ABOUT AUBERGINES

- Apart from the need for constant watering, aubergines are surprisingly easy to grow.
- They are grown from seed, in much the same way as tomatoes, cucumbers and sweet peppers.
- They can be grown outside in a sheltered corner of the garden as long as they are protected with screens – plastic screens to make the most of the sun, and net or woven willow ones to protect from cold winds.

GROWING MEDIUM

Aubergines like a rich, moist, well-drained growing medium in a sunny, sheltered position. A good option is to grow them in a bed that has been layered up with a mix of well-rotted farmyard compost, spent mushroom compost and lots of leafmould. You should have no more than four plants to a 90 cm (3 ft) square bed. Build a plastic screen to the windward side.

SOWING AND PLANTING

- **Early spring** Sow the seeds about 12 mm (½ in) deep, on a bed of moistened potting compost in a seed-tray, protect with a sheet of glass topped with newspaper, and keep warm and well watered.
- **Mid- to late spring** When the seedlings are large enough to handle, prick them out into 7.5 cm (3 in) peat pots, water and keep warm.
- **Mid- to late spring** Set the peat pots in place in the bed, water generously and protect with a plastic or net screen/shelter of your choice.

Growing medium: Rich moist well drained
Situation: Sheltered and sunny against a protective wall
Harvest: Cut away fruits with a sharp knife

GENERAL CARE

When the plant is about 30 cm (1 ft) high, remove the growing tip to encourage branching, and support with a stick. Pinch out to leave the best six fruits, and vigilantly remove subsequent flowers. Spray with water to discourage aphids. Apply a mulch of well-rotted manure and gradually remove older leaves.

HARVESTING

You can harvest between early summer and mid-autumn. When the fruits are 15–23 cm (6–9 in) long and nicely plump, slice them off with a sharp knife.

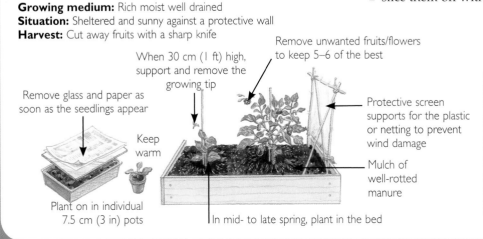

Remove glass and paper as soon as the seedlings appear

When 30 cm (1 ft) high, support and remove the growing tip

Remove unwanted fruits/flowers to keep 5–6 of the best

Keep warm

Protective screen supports for the plastic or netting to prevent wind damage

Mulch of well-rotted manure

Plant on in individual 7.5 cm (3 in) pots

In mid- to late spring, plant in the bed

Troubleshooting

Insect pests Spray the insects off with a water/liquid soap solution and then wash the leaves with plain water. Remove larger insects by hand.

Splitting fruit Prevent the problem by surrounding the plants with a mulch of well-rotted manure, and water daily.

Capsicums (Sweet peppers)

Sweet peppers are grown in much the same way as tomatoes and aubergines – they need relatively warm and sheltered conditions – but are usually easier to grow than tomatoes.

If you like salads, stir-fries and roasts with stuffed vegetables, capsicums are a good choice.

SOW   **PLANT**   **HARVEST**

mid winter	late winter	early spring	mid spring	late spring	early summer	mid summer	late summer	early autumn	mid autumn	late autumn	early winter	mid winter	late winter	early spring	mid spring	late spring	early summer	mid summer	late summer	early autumn	mid autumn	late autumn	early winter

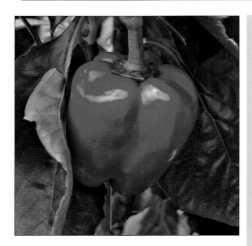

ABOUT CAPSICUMS

- Although capsicums are usually described and sold as greenhouse plants, they can, with a little bit of care, be grown in a well-sheltered spot in the open garden – perhaps against the wall of the house, or against a fence.
- You might need to use screens and / or polytunnel cloches to protect them from cold winds.
- You can sow them directly in peat pots, bring them on under glass or plastic, and then transfer them to the beds.

- A good option if a blast of cold weather is forecast is to set a wigwam of bamboo canes over the plant and wrap it around with clear plastic or bubble wrap sheeting.

GROWING MEDIUM

Capsicums do best in a well-drained, well-manured bed in a sunny, sheltered position. A good option is an extra-high raised bed with a plastic screen windbreak all around. Failing that, you could plant them in temporary bag-beds in a polytunnel or in some sort of dedicated glass or plastic shelter. If you have no choice other than to grow them in the open garden, make sure that they are in a sunny position up against a wall or fence, or perhaps against the sunny side of your shed. Load as much manure as possible on during the winter, and top it with a mulch of spent compost.

SOWING AND PLANTING

- **Late winter to early spring** Sow the seeds 18 mm (¾ in) deep in trays on a bed of moistened potting compost, and protect with a sheet of glass topped with newspaper. Keep warm.

- **Mid- to late spring** Prick out the seedlings into small peat pots. Water and keep warm.
- **Around early summer** Plant outside when the plants are strong enough. Set the peat pots directly in the bed 30–45 cm (12–18 in) apart, and protect with a cloche or plastic shelter.

GENERAL CARE

Water the seedlings before and after planting, and then daily. Every few days or so, stir the surface of the growing medium with a hoe or trowel to create a loose mulch and to keep it free from weeds and bugs. Support the plants with a cane and ties. When the plants are happily established, spread a mulch of old spent manure or straw over the bed to further hold in the moisture.

HARVESTING

You can harvest from mid-summer to mid-autumn – the actual time depends on the variety, and whether you want to pick the peppers when they are young and green or when they are well ripened and red. Use a sharp knife to cut the fruits as needed.

Growing medium: Well-manured and well-drained
Situation: Sheltered and warm/sunny against a protective wall
Harvest: Cut the fruits off with a sharp knife

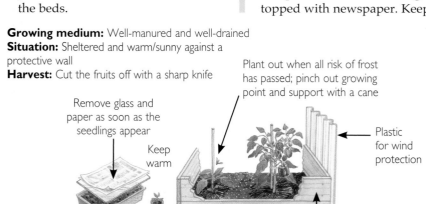

Remove glass and paper as soon as the seedlings appear

Keep warm

Plant in individual 7.5 cm (3 in) peat pots

Plant out when all risk of frost has passed; pinch out growing point and support with a cane

Plastic for wind protection

Extra frame if gales are forecast

Troubleshooting

Rolled leaves These suggest that the plants are too cold. Add a mulch of chopped straw or salvaged cardboard around the foot of the plants and protect the total bed with a screen or cover.

Mould Probably caused by virus diseases that take hold in wet and cold conditions. Remove affected fruit and leaves. Wash the plant with a solution of liquid soap and water, and rake up and remove the top 2.5 cm (1 in) or so of growing medium. If the problem persists, spray with an organic anti-mould drench.

Culinary herbs

Herbs are perfect for your no-dig garden. What could be better than gathering all the makings for a meal, and rounding it off by picking a handful or two of fresh herbs?

GETTING STARTED

Good advice when thinking about planting herbs in no-dig beds is to start with the most familiar items such as mint, parsley, chives and sage, and go for the more unusual herbs when time allows. It is best to plant in small dedicated beds so that you can shape the growing medium – varying amounts of compost and manure – to suit the specific needs of each herb, and so that you can control the spreading and invasive habits of herbs like mint.

HERBS

- **Bay** A hardy evergreen shrub with dark green, aromatic leaves. In ideal conditions, it can grow to a height of 1.8–3.5 m (6–12 ft), and likes a well-drained, moisture-retentive medium in a sunny position. The leaves give a rich flavour to stews and fish dishes.
- **Borage** A hardy annual with oval, slightly hairy, green leaves. It grows to a height of about 90 cm (3 ft), and likes a well-drained, moisture-retentive medium in full sun. The leaves can be added to cold drinks and used in salads.
- **Chervil** A hardy biennial that is usually grown as an annual, with bright green, fern-like leaves – they look a bit like parsley. It grows to a height of about 45 cm (18 in), and prefers a rich, moderately moist growing medium in a sunny position. The delicate aniseed-flavoured leaves are good in salads and sandwiches, and with fish and egg dishes.
- **Chives** A hardy, low-growing, clump-forming perennial with green, tubular stems topped with round, rose-pink flowerheads. Chives do best in a rich growing medium in a sheltered, sunny corner, and they need to be regularly watered. The chopped-up stems and leaves have a beautifully distinctive, tart, onion-like flavour that is good in sandwiches and omelettes.
- **Dill** A hardy annual with tall stems topped with feathery, blue-green leaves. It grows to a height of 60–90 cm (2–3 ft), and thrives in a well-drained, moderately fertile growing medium in a sheltered, sunny position. The freshly picked leaves are used to best effect to garnish and flavour new potatoes and white fish.
- **Fennel** A hardy herbaceous perennial with tall stems, feathery, green leaves and golden-yellow flowerheads. It grows to a height of 1.5–1.8 m (5–6 ft), and does best in a moist, well-drained, moderately fertile growing medium in a sheltered, sunny position. The leaves are good with fish, salads and stews, while the seeds add taste and texture to cakes, breads and soups.
- **Mint** Common mint is a hardy herbaceous perennial with mid-green leaves. It grows to a height of about 60 cm (2 ft), and does well in a moisture-retentive, fertile growing medium in a warm, sheltered position. The leaves are perfect when chopped with brown sugar and used with vinegar in the form of a mint sauce, or simply picked and added to boiled new potatoes.
- **Parsley** A hardy biennial that tends to be grown as an annual, with curly, tightly packed, green leaves. It does best in a moisture-retentive, fertile growing medium in full sun or shade. The leaves are commonly used in sauces and as a garnish.
- **Rosemary** An evergreen shrub with narrow, spiky, mid- to dark green, aromatic leaves that will grow just about anywhere. The leaves are used to flavour a range of fish and meat dishes.
- **Sage** A hardy evergreen shrub with long, aromatic, green-grey leaves. It thrives in a fertile growing medium in a warm, sheltered spot. The leaves are extensively used in a range of dishes from sage-and-onion stuffing to cheese-sage dip, and taste really good in a nut roast.
- **Thyme** A hardy, dwarf, evergreen shrub with small, aromatic leaves. It grows best in a light, well-drained growing medium in an airy, sunny position. The leaves are good with fish and rich meats such as hare and pork.

If you are short of room, you can grow beautiful and tasty herbs wherever there is space among your flowers and shrubs.

Strawberries

With as few as 20 strawberry plants, during the fruiting season you should be able to pick plenty enough to eat every day, give some to relations and neighbours, and make jam. Colourful, juicy strawberries are an absolute joy, especially when picked and eaten fresh immediately.

PLANT BARE-ROOTED (Plant container-grown any time)   **HARVEST**   **PRUNE**

mid winter	late winter	early spring	mid spring	late spring	early summer	mid summer	late summer	early autumn	mid autumn	late autumn	early winter	mid winter	late winter	early spring	mid spring	late spring	early summer	mid summer	late summer	early autumn	mid autumn	late autumn	early winter

ABOUT STRAWBERRIES

- Although strawberry types are described in the catalogues as 'perpetual', 'wild' and other names, they actually break down into early, mid-season and late varieties.
- Strawberries do best when they are grown en masse, say four to a 90 cm (3 ft) square bed.
- You can plant strawberries in late summer, mid-autumn to early winter, and spring. Only summer planting is described here, but the basics apply for all planting times.
- Strawberries can easily be propagated by layering the runners, about three from each plant, into pots or straight into the growing medium.

GROWING MEDIUM

Strawberries thrive in a well-manured bed in a sunny position with some shelter or screen to the windward side.

PLANTING (SUMMER)

- Fill the bed with plenty of well-rotted manure and/or garden compost.
- In mid-summer to early autumn, for bare-rooted plants, dig shallow holes wide enough to take the roots at full spread, say four plants in a 90 cm (3 ft) square bed.
- Carefully spread the roots out to their full extent, top the holes up with well-rotted garden compost and friable soil, ease and lift the plant slightly, and press firmly so that the crown is just above ground level. Gently 'puddle' plants into place.

GENERAL CARE

When the fruits start to form, keep up the watering and spread a thick mulch of fresh straw around the plants to keep them warm and clean, and to hold back the weeds. Push in sticks or wires to make a low bowed support, and spread a net over them to keep off the birds.

HARVESTING

Pick the strawberries as they ripen, as soon as the colour is uniform. The best time is early morning when the berries are dry. Pick the berries complete with the stalks and plugs. It is best if the fruit is eaten or cooked on the day of picking.

Growing medium: Fertile and well-drained
Situation: Sunny
Harvest: Stalk and plug when evenly red

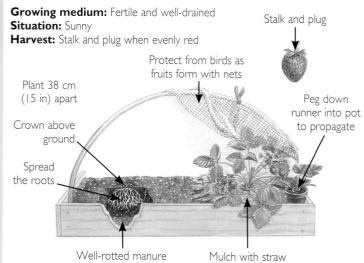

Stalk and plug

Protect from birds as fruits form with nets

Plant 38 cm (15 in) apart

Peg down runner into pot to propagate

Crown above ground

Spread the roots

Well-rotted manure

Mulch with straw

Troubleshooting

Slugs and snails Damage shows as slimy bites and holes in the fruit. Remove the pests by hand.

Mould and mildew This shows as limp, mouldy foliage and fruit drop. Clean up and remove the debris, and drench the plants with an organic mould spray. Once fruiting is over, cut off the foliage, gather all the straw mulch and debris and burn the lot. This helps to keep diseases down. Avoid the problem next time by growing a disease-resistant variety in a different bed in a well-ventilated, sunny spot.

Blackened flowers Probably frost or wind damage. Avoid the problem by covering with a fine fleece if a cold spell is forecast and by watering the ground rather than the plants.

Raspberries

Raspberries and their close hybrid cousins loganberries, veitchberries and lowberries are a good option for a medium-sized no-dig garden. Choose a suitable variety (summer- or autumn-fruiting, vigorous, restrained growth, heavy-fruiting, disease-resistant) to match your requirements.

(Plant container-grown any time) **PLANT BARE-ROOTED** **PRUNE** **HARVEST** **PRUNE**

mid winter	late winter	early spring	mid spring	late spring	early summer	mid summer	late summer	early autumn	mid autumn	late autumn	early winter	mid winter	late winter	early spring	mid spring	late spring	early summer	mid summer	late summer	early autumn	mid autumn	late autumn	early winter

ABOUT RASPBERRIES

- The raspberry is a hardy deciduous shrub – a member of the rose family.
- There are two kinds of raspberries – those that fruit in the summer and those that fruit in the autumn.
- The tender fruits should be eaten raw or cooked on the day of picking.

GROWING MEDIUM

Although generally summer- and autumn-fruiting raspberries have much the same needs – a well-drained bed with plenty of rotted manure in a well-sheltered, sunny position, away from draughts and deep shade – autumn-fruiting raspberries need just that bit more sun, air and shelter. A good option in an existing no-dig raised bed garden is to convert a number of side-by-side square beds into a single long, narrow bed to give you a bed about 90 cm (3 ft) wide by 1.8–3.5 m (6–12 ft) long.

PLANTING

- **Late autumn to early winter** For bare-rooted canes, dig a trench 30 cm (1 ft) deep and 45 cm (18 in) wide (length to suit you) and half-fill it with well-rotted farmyard manure. Set the bare-rooted canes in place about 38 cm (15 in) apart.
- Fill the trench with a mix of garden compost and old manure and tread firm. Cut the canes down to about 30 cm (1 ft) from the ground.
- Along the length of the bed, build a support frame or fence that has horizontal wires at 60 cm (2 ft), 90 cm (3 ft) and 1.5 m (5 ft) from the ground.

GENERAL CARE

Summer-fruiting varieties In spring, when young canes start to grow, cut the old dead wood down to ground level. Tie the new growing canes to the support wires. After fruiting, cut all fruiting canes down to ground level, and tie up all the new canes.

Autumn-fruiting varieties After fruiting, cut all the canes down to ground level.

HARVESTING

Pick the raspberries on a dry, sunny day, as soon as they are fully coloured. Snip them off complete with the stalk, or pull the fruit clear of the stalks. Remove, gather and burn the debris.

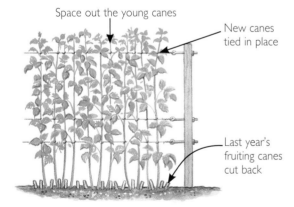

Space out the young canes

New canes tied in place

Last year's fruiting canes cut back

Troubleshooting

Curling leaf aphids Damage shows as curled edges to the leaves, premature fruit fall and general weakening of the canes. Drench with an organic spray, wash with clean water and remove the mess from the surface of the bed. At the end of the season, spray the canes with winter wash and burn the debris.

Maggoty fruit Most likely raspberry beetles, which feed on the flowers and lay eggs that eventually produce grubs that attack the berries. Avoid the problem next time by burning old canes as soon as they are cut, generally clearing up rubbish, and spraying with a winter wash at the end of the season.

Blackberries

There is no doubt that blackberries are easy to grow and fruitful – an average plant will give 4.5–11 kg (10–25 lb) of fruit – but you will need lots of space. Blackberries can be eaten fresh or used in desserts, jams, juices and sauces. They also make a good cough syrup.

PLANT BARE-ROOTED (Plant container-grown any time)　　　**PRUNE**　　　**HARVEST**

mid winter	late winter	early spring	mid spring	late spring	early summer	mid summer	late summer	early autumn	mid autumn	late autumn	early winter	mid winter	late winter	early spring	mid spring	late spring	early summer	mid summer	late summer	early autumn	mid autumn	late autumn	early winter

ABOUT BLACKBERRIES

- Most people know a blackberry when they see one. In the UK and many parts of Europe, collecting wild blackberries is a traditional activity that can evoke strong memories of childhood, rural hardship and wartime food shortages.
- There are small, thornless varieties that are good for small gardens.
- Blackberries can be grown more or less anywhere, as long as there is plenty of sun and dry air.

GROWING MEDIUM

Blackberries thrive in just about any growing medium as long as it is well manured, free from standing water and of a good depth. In a no-dig raised bed garden, they do best when planted as free-standing clumps so that they receive all-round sun.

PLANTING

- In late autumn to early winter for bare-rooted canes, and at any time for container-grown ones, dig a hole that is 23 cm (9 in) deep and 60 cm (2 ft) wide. Spread about 10 cm (4 in) of well-rotted manure in the bottom of the hole and set the bare-rooted canes or container-grown plants in place so that the roots are only just covered. Fill the hole with well-rotted manure and top with compacted mushroom compost or garden compost.

- Build a 1.8 m (6 ft) high post-and-wire support frame, with horizontal wires at 30 cm (1 ft) intervals.

GENERAL CARE

After planting, cut down the canes to about 23 cm (9 in) above the bed – each cut should be just above a strong, healthy bud. During the first summer, weave and train the young canes along all but the top wire. In the second year, train the new canes up through to the top wire. In the autumn, cut down all fruiting canes. Repeat the procedure in all following years.

HARVESTING

Pick the berries when the colour has just changed from red to black, while they are still firm. As a test, take a berry and gently ease it away – if it comes cleanly away from its plug and stalk, it is ready. Blackberries need to be eaten fresh on the day of picking or swiftly bottled or frozen.

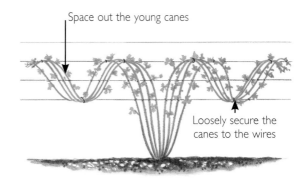

Space out the young canes

Loosely secure the canes to the wires

Troubleshooting

Sticky curling leaves These indicate aphids. Large colonies of aphids will result in distorted shoots and fruit drop. Minimize the problem by burning all the cuttings and debris at the end of the season. Avoid it next time by spraying with a winter oil wash to destroy the aphid eggs.

Grey mould This shows itself as a grey-white powder on the foliage, indicating humid, stale-air, cold conditions. Avoid the problem by cutting back the lower foliage to let in the air, and by generally clearing away all the debris on the ground.

Currants (black, red and white)

Although each of the currants needs slightly different treatment, they are grouped together here because most people think of them as being very similar. Blackcurrants are more popular than either red or white currants.

| PLANT BARE-ROOTED | | (Plant container-grown any time) | | | | | | | | PRUNE | | | | | | | HARVEST | | | | | |

mid winter	late winter	early spring	mid spring	late spring	early summer	mid summer	late summer	early autumn	mid autumn	late autumn	early winter	mid winter	late winter	early spring	mid spring	late spring	early summer	mid summer	late summer	early autumn	mid autumn	late autumn	early winter

ABOUT CURRANTS

- Blackcurrants need to be treated differently from red and white currants, and they are easier to grow and care for.
- Blackcurrants are usually made into jam, while red and white currants tend to be made into sauces and jellies.
- While red and white currants can be trained up wires, in a no-dig raised bed garden it is easiest to grow all three types as bush forms.

GROWING MEDIUM

Currants do best in a well-drained, deeply worked, well-manured growing medium. Select a deep bed, break up the hard subsoil and layer up with alternate mulches of farmyard manure, leafmould and garden compost. The ideal site is moist but well-drained, sunny with a good circulation of air, and with some protection to the windward side.

PLANTING

- Plant in late autumn, or late winter to early spring, for bare-rooted bushes, and at any time for container-grown bushes.
- Dig a hole that is plenty wide and deep enough for the roots to spread out.
- Spread about 10 cm (4 in) of well-rotted manure over the bottom of the hole and set the bare-rooted or container-grown plant in place. Backfill and make adjustments so that the ground mark on the stem is level with the surface of the growing medium within the bed.
- Fill the hole up with well-rotted manure topped with well-compacted garden compost.

GENERAL CARE

After planting blackcurrants, cut all stems down to about 2.5 cm (1 in) above soil level, and in the following season cut out all shoots that have produced fruit. With red and white currants, cut the main shoots back by half immediately after planting. In late winter, cut out shoots that cross the plant's centre. When the fruit starts to form, protect the whole bush with fine netting to keep off the birds.

HARVESTING

Pick the fruit immediately after the colour has turned, while the berries are still firm and shiny. Pick off the whole cluster rather than individual berries. In a good year, you might need to do this once or twice a week.

Blackcurrant, first season after pruning

Red or white currant, pruned as a bush

Troubleshooting

Vanishing berries Birds will strip the bushes bare if you give them a chance. Avoid the problem by covering the beds with nets or by growing the bushes in a netted cage.

Holes in leaves and distorted shoots Probably caused by capsid bugs. Spray with a winter wash and avoid the problem next time by growing a resistant variety.

Gooseberries

In earlier times, gooseberries eaten raw straight off the bush were very bristly and sharp in taste, but once they were topped, tailed, cooked and served up as pies, crumbles and jam they were wonderful. Some modern dessert varieties are described as being good eaten raw.

PRUNE ▽ **PLANT BARE-ROOTED** ▽ (Plant container-grown any time) **HARVEST** ▽

mid winter	late winter	early spring	mid spring	late spring	early summer	mid summer	late summer	early autumn	mid autumn	late autumn	early winter	mid winter	late winter	early spring	mid spring	late spring	early summer	mid summer	late summer	early autumn	mid autumn	late autumn	early winter

ABOUT GOOSEBERRIES

- Gooseberries seem to do well against all the odds. A totally neglected bush will give a surprising amount of fruit, but picking will be difficult.
- Although the gooseberry is generally the first fruit to be ready for use, it is seldom seen in shops – all the more reason perhaps to grow your own.

GROWING MEDIUM

Gooseberries thrive in just about any deeply dug, well-manured growing medium. Although they will grow in a dank corner of the garden, they will be more susceptible to moulds and blights than when they are grown in a light, sunny corner. The ideal is a bed that is moist but well-drained, with plenty of well-rotted manure to hold in the moisture, situated in a sunny, open, airy spot that is sheltered on the cold, windward sides.

PLANTING

- Plant in mid- to late autumn, or late winter to early spring, for bare-rooted bushes, and at any time for container-grown ones.
- Dig a hole that is plenty wide and deep enough for the roots to spread out.
- Spread about 10 cm (4 in) of well-rotted manure over the bottom of the hole and set the bare-rooted or container-grown plants in place. Ease container-grown plants from their pots and arrange them so that they are level with the growing medium.
- Fill the hole up with a mix of well-rotted manure topped with well-compacted garden compost.

GENERAL CARE

After planting, cut back each main branch by about half. In the following autumn, cut back by half all the shoots that have formed in the year. At the end of the following season, shorten those shoots produced during the season by half and clear out any shoots that crowd out the centre. An open framework will make picking easier.

HARVESTING

Pick fruit for cooking as soon as it starts to colour and while it is still hard, and fruit for eating when it feels slightly soft to the touch. In a good year, you might need to gather the fruit once or twice a week. Trim off the tough tops and tails.

← Shorten the young shoots in the first and second seasons, so that you have a well-shaped bush

Troubleshooting

Curling, distorted leaves Probably caused by aphids. Spray them off with organic spray, wash the resulting mess off with water, and in winter spray with an organic wash.

Holes in leaves These are usually the work of one of the fly pests. At the end of the season, remove all the surface of the bed to a depth of 7.5–10 cm (3–4 in) and burn it, and spray with an organic winter wash. Be careful not to burn the roots that are just under the surface of the bed.

Rhubarb

Fresh rhubarb stalks picked, cooked and eaten straight from the garden are tender, sweet and altogether beautiful, a real treat. The good news is that most children love garden rhubarb, especially when it is dished up with custard, yogurt or ice cream, or best of all made into a crumble.

PLANT ROOT   **HARVEST**

mid winter	late winter	early spring	mid spring	late spring	early summer	mid summer	late summer	early autumn	mid autumn	late autumn	early winter	mid winter	late winter	early spring	mid spring	late spring	early summer	mid summer	late summer	early autumn	mid autumn	late autumn	early winter

ABOUT RHUBARB

- Rhubarb is a vegetable that we treat as a fruit.
- Although rhubarb can be raised from seed, the swiftest and most common method of propagating is by root division.
- Although the plants can be grown in the same bed for 20 years or so, most keen gardeners replant every 5–10 years.
- The leaves contain high levels of toxic chemicals. Cut them off and put them on the compost heap.

GROWING MEDIUM

The ideal growing medium is a deep, rich loam that is cool, moist and well-drained. Rhubarb does not like boggy, waterlogged soil. In preparation, the beds should be generously layered up in autumn with plenty of manure. The ideal site for early varieties is warm and well drained, with protection from cold winds, with the ground sloping towards the sun. Later varieties can stand a more open position and a heavier growing medium. Although rhubarb needs plenty of moisture all through the growing season, and although a low, boggy situation is unsuitable, a very dry soil is equally bad.

PLANTING

- **Late winter to early spring** Plant divided dormant roots in ground that has been previously manured. Dig a 30 cm (1 ft) deep hole wide enough to take the spread of the roots. Set the plants 75 cm (30 in) apart, in rows 90 cm (3 ft) apart.
- Fill around the root with a mix of garden compost and old manure so that the growing tips are just showing, and firm.

Growing medium: Deep, rich and moist
Situation: Sunny and sheltered
Harvest: Pull at base, twisting up and out by hand

Forcing for early crop: Use upturned bucket, box or terracotta forcer to cover the dormant buds

Forced rhubarb

Remove flowers

Planted so the bud is just above the surface

Protect with straw in winter

Mulch

Trim and compost both ends

Compost and spent manure

Manure

GENERAL CARE

As soon as planting is complete, stir the surface of the bed to reduce compaction and cover the ground with a generous mulch of well-rotted manure. Water as often as possible. Remove flower stems as soon as they appear. Encourage an early crop by covering the plants with straw and black plastic sheet.

HARVESTING

Gather the stalks from early spring to mid-summer. Grip one stalk at a time close to the ground and give it a half-turn 'yank' so that it comes away from the crown. Use a sharp knife to trim both ends of the stalk – the leaf at one end and the white piece at the other. Toss the debris on the compost heap and move on to the next stalk.

Troubleshooting

Crown rot This shows as a squashy brown area on the side of the crown, with the stalks and shoots looking generally weak and scrawny. Crown rot can devastate a bed, so burn the plants as soon as the disease shows and grow a completely different variety in a bed at the other end of the garden.

Tip rot Avoid the problem by making sure that the tips are always visible.

Pests and diseases

How can I keep plants healthy?

Apart from a number of very good home-made organic sprays, meaning recipes like a chopped tomato leaves soaked in water that can sprayed on aphids, and a chopped garlic and oil mix that is a great antibacterial, antifungal and insect pest spray, a very efficient way forward is to cover the crops with fleece, netting and such like, so as to create physical barriers to keep insect and animals pests at bay.

ABOVE-GROUND PESTS AND DISEASES – SYMPTOMS AND CONTROLS

Birds

Cause damage to plants – protect with nets, or better still plant extra crops for the birds in the knowledge that some birds are beneficial in that they will eat insect pests.

Slugs and snails

Cause slimy damage to leaves and stalks – remove by hand. Some gardeners advocate ringing the beds with a copper wire stripped from an electric cable, their thinking being that something about the copper – perhaps the heat, or electric shock, or copper oxide – keeps the slimy pests away.

Cabbage caterpillars

Seen as holes, eggs and actual caterpillars – protect with fine nets to keep off the butterflies, and collect and destroy the eggs and the caterpillars.

Diamond-back moths

Show themselves as caterpillars feeding on the underside of leaves – protect with nets to keep of the moths and collect the caterpillars by hand.

Green capsid bugs

Makes holes in leaves and deforms growth – drench with organic spray.

Red spider mites

Causes the leafy veins of leaves to turn yellow-red-brown and results in a dusty covering – control by drenching with Neem oil (an organic pesticide), or with a homemade coriander and oil spray.

Earwigs

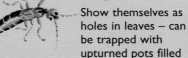

Show themselves as holes in leaves – can be trapped with upturned pots filled with straw and controlled with garlic and pepper spray.

Greenhouse whitefly

Shows as a sticky mess of eggs on the underside of leaves and as deformed leaves – spray with insect soap or dust with seaweed powder.

Mosaic virus

Shows as spotted green-yellow areas on the leaves and eventually results in complete plant failure – drench with a tobacco and water spray and burn badly damaged plants.

Asparagus beetles

Cause damage to leaves and stems – collect and destroy the beetles, grubs and all the debris.

Flea beetles

Cause small holes in leaves – drench with garlic and oil spray and burn debris.

Rust

Reveals itself as a brown scab-like condition on leaves – garlic and oil spray seems to work, as does a spray made from Neem oil. Limit the problem by burning all the debris at the end of the season.

Tomato leaf mould

Reveals itself as yellow-brown leaves and wilting plant. Remove damaged leaves and drench the plants with a mix of water, baking soda, veg oil and dishwashing liquid.

Aphids (greenfly)

Sticky mess indicates an infestation – drench with garlic and pepper spray and burn debris.

Smut

Shows on the leaves as a sooty looking mess that smears on contact – very difficult to control. Wash off with a thin soapy spray, and/or drench with a Neem oil spray. Burn all the debris at the end of the season and do your best to avoid the problem the next time around by planting resistant varieties on a different bed.

Mice

Cause damage to crops – especially peas – by eating seeds, munching pods and generally being a nuisance. Having tried traps, paraffin, mesh and nets, I now sow peas in the greenhouse in lengths of plastic gutter, wait until they are about 2-3 inches high, slide the young plants into place in the beds and then follow on by ringing the beds around with nets.

Black bean aphids

Show themselves as a mess of sticky black aphids on leaves and stems – drench with a mix of soft soap and white mineral oil, and do your best to encourage predatory ladybugs and other aphid-eating wildlife.

Pea and bean weevils

Cause damage as they bite and nibble around the edges of the leaves – puff organic derris dust around the leaves and burn all the ground debris.

Pea thrips

Result in silvery brown misshaped pods – spray with insecticidal soap – avoid the problem by burning all the debris.

Pea moths

Cause maggoty peas – guard against by ringing the bed with a barrier of fine fleece or netting – drench with a natural soap spray.

Potato blight

Shows as black and brown spots on leaves and scabby soft potatoes – very difficult to control, the best option is to clear the beds, burn the debris, and next time around to plant resistant varieties on a new bed.

Potato leaf roll virus

Reveals itself as rolled edges to the leaves – drench with an anti-aphid mix, and use a resistant variety the next time around.

Bean halo blight

Causes squashy rusty scabs on the leaves and eventual plant failure – first try an organic spray, and if this fails pull and burn the plants, and next time around plant disease resistant varieties on new beds.

Powdery mildew

Shows as a flour-like dusting on leaves – drench with milk and water spray.

Celery heart rot

Causes a soft brown rot at the centre or heart of the plant – avoid by binding the growing plant up tight with raffia and gradually earthing the growing plants up so that the stalks are hidden from view, and the centre of the plant is free from standing water

Celery leaf miners

Causes brown blistering and shrivelling of the leaves – collect and kill the larvae, and drench the plants with a soft soap solution. Earth up to minimize the problem.

HOME-MADE ORGANIC SPRAYS

Be aware that in some countries it is illegal in some instances to make some home-made traditional recipes for insect and pest control.

- **Garlic and pepper** – add 3 cloves crushed garlic and 1 tablespoon vegetable oil to 3 tablespoons hot pepper sauce; let it stand overnight. Next add the mix to 1 small spoonful unscented washing-up liquid and add it all to 4 cups water. This mix can be sprayed direct as it is.

- **Garlic and oil** – add 3 cloves crushed garlic to 2 small spoonfuls mineral oil, let it sit for a day, then strain and add to 0.5 litre (1 pint) water. Shake and add 1 small spoonful washing-up liquid. When you come to spray, add 2 tablespoons of this mix to 0.5 litre (1 pint) water.

- **Tomato leaf** – soak 2 cups chopped tomato leaves in 2 cups water, leave overnight and strain. When you spray, use 1 measure of the mix to 1 of water.

- **Insecticidal soap** – 1 small spoonful pure unscented soap mixed with 1 litre (2 pints) water – dissolves insects like aphids, mites, thrips and a whole range of scale insects.

- **Neem oil** – Neem seed oil repels cabbage worm, aphids, moth larvae, and also control powdery mildew and rust. 25 g (1 oz) Neem oil and a few drops soap liquid mixed into 4 litres (1 gallon) water makes a good spray to treat all manner of mould and mites.

BELOW-GROUND PESTS AND DISEASES – SYMPTOMS AND CONTROLS

Slugs and snails

Signs are slimy trails and general damage to roots, fruits, shoots and indeed everything. Slugs and snails dislike barriers of wood ash, crushed eggshells, human and pet hair, oat bran and sprigs of rosemary spread around plants. Another good barrier method is to staple a continuous loop of copper wire around the top of the wooden bed. You can also try slug 'traps', such as a sunken receptacle containing a little beer into which the pests fall and drown.

Warning

It is a good idea with all plant sprays – whether they be home-made, handed down, traditional or shop-bought – to have a trial run by spraying just a little on a single plant to see if it works or does damage. You must approach all sprays and cures with the assumption that they might be dangerous – meaning you must wear gloves, a mask and goggles, and you must wash your skin on contact, and safely label or dispose of all left-overs.

Woodlice

Little hard-coated lice that can often be seen crawling and rolling up into balls. They cause damage by chewing roots and seedlings. Remove and burn all the debris from around the plants, rake the ground to disturb the woodlice, and drench with a mix of mild detergent and vegetable oil – 1 part oil and a dash of liquid soap to 100 parts water.

Cabbage root fly

You will notice small white maggots in the soil and general damage to roots. The plants will wilt and die. Dust organic derris powder around the roots, and burn the plants at the end of the season.

Millipedes

Many-legged millipedes cause damage to roots. They can be trapped in cans filled with carrot or potato peelings, or sprayed with a garlic and pepper mix.

Crown and stem rot

You will see a soft, brown mess around the lower stem, and general wilting. Horseradish spray seems to work. Add 1 cup liquidized horseradish to 475 ml (16 fl oz) water and let it soak overnight. Strain off the liquid and mix it with 2 litres (4 pints) water. The resulting mix is a good spray for a whole range of fungal diseases.

Root rot

This is caused by various fungal diseases, shows as soggy, brown roots and general wilting. Burn damaged plants and avoid the problem next time by choosing a bed that is extra well drained and by increasing the amount of compost.

Cutworms

These are caterpillars of various moths. Symptoms show as chewed and eaten stems and roots. A sprinkling of cornmeal or bran scattered throughout the garden will kill cutworms, which munch it up and die.

Clubroot

This first shows as wart-like nodules on the roots, and the plant eventually wilts and dies. There is no cure for clubroot. Burn the diseased crops as soon as possible, and next time plant resistant varieties in different beds.

Wireworms

Green larvae of click beetles, which cause general damage to roots, stems and tubers. A garlic and oil spray works really well.

Leatherjackets

These are the fat legless grubs of craneflies (also know as 'daddy-long-legs'), which cause general damage to roots. Spray the ground with a water and liquid soap mix. Bear in mind that, while the grubs do most certainly damage roots, this might be offset by the fact that the adult flies eat aphids, mites and leafhoppers.

Cockchafer grubs

You may see larvae feeding on roots and tubers, and/or damage to roots and tubers. Remove and burn all debris, and then spray with a garlic and oil mix.

Root-knot eelworms

These first show themselves as galls and deforming nodules on the roots of many vegetables, and then finally as stunted growth. Remove damaged roots, leave the soil for three weeks and drench with a mix of molasses or sugar and water. Research suggests that adding a mulch of fresh chicken manure can help to reduce the problem.

Troubleshooting

Clearing an area of the garden, building raised beds, filling the beds with various mixes of farmyard manure, garden compost and spent mushroom compost, planting up the beds, and battling with nature to achieve maximum cropping all make for an engaging experience. One year it might be all success, and the next you might have problems, but this is why growing vegetables is such a great challenge.

NO-DIG RAISED BED TROUBLESHOOTING

QUESTION	ANSWER
The basic plot is completely overgrown with weeds – an old lawn that has gone to ruin. How do I start?	Cut down and burn as many of the weeds as possible. Pull up and burn plants like nettles, thistles and docks, and then cover the whole plot with black plastic sheeting.
I have spent weeks building the beds and getting them into place, but weeds are springing up in the path areas. What can I do?	As soon as the beds are sorted and in place, cover the path areas with black plastic sheeting, old carpets, old plastic sacks, or anything that will starve the weeds of sunlight, and then spread a thick mulch of woodchip over the paths.
I am building the beds from 23 x 5 cm (9 x 2 in) rough-sawn and treated timber (as shown on page 7), but I think that some beds need to be deeper. What can I do?	The easiest option is to build more frames as already described – with the same internal dimensions – only this time make them from less expensive 15 x 2.5 cm (6 x 1 in) section timber. In this way you will be able to increase the depth of your beds by multiples of 15 cm (6 in).
Why do you describe the soil as 'growing medium'?	The word 'soil' defines the natural ground, meaning the top layer of the earth's surface that is made up of rock, mineral particles and organic matter. The content of the beds is a mix of brought-in materials, so it is not true soil. The term 'growing medium' underlines the fact that it has to be created and formulated.
What do you think is a good mix for filling the beds?	Equal parts of spent mushroom compost, fresh farmyard manure, well-rotted farmyard manure, garden compost and poultry manure. Then you can use poultry manure, garden compost and the occasion load of horse manure as mulches. (Avoid the temptation to use bought-in 'topsoil' in the beds, as this will contain weed seeds.)
We have a sloping site, so how can we best place the beds?	Use a spirit-level to ensure that they are true and level and you finish up with a sort of stepped terrace of beds. Depending upon the pitch of the slope, you will have to dig one side of the bed into the natural ground slightly, and/or prop the other side up. You can use bricks to prop up the lower side of the bed until the spirit-level shows it is level, place and screw another length of plank to the propped-up side of the bed, and remove the bricks.
Can I shape the beds in height and width to suit my physical disability?	Just about everything about the beds can be modified apart from the width – the 90 cm (3 ft) width is necessary so that you can work it from both sides without actually standing on the growing medium. If you can stretch but have trouble bending, you could increase the height of the beds so that the growing surface is at a comfortable level. You could increase the width of the paths to allow for a wheelchair, pram or motor barrow.
How can I protect against butterflies?	The easiest option is to insert a couple of plastic water-pipe half-hoops over the bed, and then cover with very fine netting or even a found product such as net curtain, so that you finish up with a miniature polytunnel-like structure. In this way you can stop the butterflies before they ever get to lay their eggs.
Could I make the sides of the beds from small bales of straw?	You can make the sides of the beds from just about any found item or material that takes your fancy – wood, brick, stone, concrete, rigid plastic sheet, galvanized sheeting, bales of straw. The only proviso is that the product or material is long-lasting and adaptable. So straw bales are fine as long as you do not mind replacing them every year or so when they rot and break down. If and when the bales break down, however, you could add them to the beds as mulch – a very nice recycling touch.

NO-DIG RAISED BED TROUBLESHOOTING

QUESTION	ANSWER
I have covered the paths with plastic sheet topped with a layer of woodchip, just as you described. What shall I do with the woodchip when it starts to rot and break down?	Woodchip is a winner on the paths on many counts: it is firm underfoot, it is not slippery, it can easily be weeded, it can be ordered in bulk, and when it rots and breaks down it can be spread on the beds as a thin mulch, and replaced. It fits beautifully into the organic, no-dig, recycling theme.
What can I do about mice eating my peas?	Sow the seeds in the greenhouse in a length of plastic gutter (as described on page 25). When the plants are 5–7.5 cm (2–3 in) high, slide the pea plants into place in the prepared beds, and surround the bed with a fine net. You could also set two traps in each bed, and generally keep watch.
Is it true that I can keep my runner bean plants from one year to the next?	Although most people plant beans as annuals, they are in fact perennials. This being so, you can achieve early crops of runner beans by digging up the roots in autumn when the crops have been gathered in, and saving them for replanting in the following spring. Wait until the runner beans have died down, cut the old dry foliage down to about 7.5 cm (3 in) from the ground and use a fork to carefully lift out the roots. Wash the roots and bring them indoors so that they are cool and dry. Plant the roots out in spring and treat as for sown beans.
Your 'distance apart' measurements seem very much closer than in traditional vegetable gardening. Why is this?	The no-dig raised bed system mimics nature in that the largely undisturbed growing medium is packed full of beneficial organisms and in near-perfect condition, and you can walk right around the bed so that there is no need to walk between lines of plants, so it is possible to set the plants closer together. The ideal is to space the plants so that the mature crop completely covers the bed and you cannot see the growing medium.
Does it matter how we align the crops with the sun?	Much depends on the location of your plot, the shape of the land, and how the plot is shaded. For example, we live in the UK on a sloping site that is shaded by large trees on the western boundary. So the plot gets full benefit of the sun right from sunrise through to late afternoon, and from then on in the plot is in the shade. This being so, we try to arrange things so that lines of tall plants such as runner beans run from east to west – so that at least the lines get to have sun on both sides. The orientation of small, low plants like courgettes is not so important, as long as they are not overshadowed by taller plants. The whole object of the exercise is to try to ensure that all the plants get their fair share of the sun.
Last year my parsnips took so long to come through that the bed spent weeks looking empty and bare. Could I have planted some sort of temporary crop to fill the space?	Yes, the best advice with a slow-growing crop like parsnips is to intercrop (see page 20) with something that you know is going to swiftly grow up and be finished before the parsnips really get going, such as radishes and salad leaves.
My large 90 cm (36 in) square wooden compost bins are completely full and there is too much compost to use this year. Can I plant them up with courgettes?	Good idea. Simply top off your compost bins with a good 15 cm (6 in) of well-rotted farmyard manure and plant them there. You should get a lovely crop!
My leeks became lanky and did not do very well over winter. What should I do next time?	The best option is to plant them in holes as described on page 54, and then gradually add additional bed frames and layers of mulch, so that by the time the leeks are fully grown they are more or less buried. This technique supports the plants as they grow, increases the quality of the growing medium, and protects the plants so that they can better survive a difficult cold winter.
Is there any swift and easy way of stopping slugs and snails from attacking my raised beds?	Like most gardeners, we have tried everything from slug pellets, broken egg shells, beer in jam jars, to stretched cotton wiped with garlic, and so on. What seems to work best is copper wire (although why it works is a mystery). Strip the copper wire out leftover power cable (maybe begged from friends and neighbours) and then staple the lengths so that the tops of the beds are completely ringed. The slugs and snails slide up to the copper, give it a look over and then slide off.
Is it really worth all the effort of keeping poultry just to ensure a steady supply of manure?	There is no denying that keeping poultry is a bit of a chore, but there are many more pros than cons. You will have as many fresh eggs as you can eat, you will be able to give eggs to friends and family, the poultry nicely takes care of gluts of fruit, salad, cabbages and so on, and you will have as much organic manure as you can handle. Keeping poultry nicely completes the growing, eating, waste and recycling loop. Just think – you could be eating freshly picked courgettes from the garden and fresh eggs all swiftly fried in olive oil and served up with lumps of new brown bread!

Index